The Creative Corridor

Global Gateway for Marketing Innovation

Kanu Chauhan

Acknowledgement

A special thanks to all of my teachers in whichever institute they are currently working. You have all imparted great knowledge to me. I respect you all and pay great thanks for educating me and considering me capable enough to set my own path.

A big chunk of thanks to my editor and publisher, Panda Publishing Agency UK for giving me the best platform possible to live my dream through you guys. I am glad we have collaborated. And I hope we go far!

Last but not least, obviously, goes to my readers! If you have read my book, it means I will probably shed a tear of joy somewhere in the corner of the world. You are now attached to my world, journey, and my emotions. Thanks for letting me be a tiny part of your world, wherever in this world you are, my sweet reader.

Welcome, Reader, to a Journey of Creativity and Innovation

Step into the vibrant heartbeat of London with me—a city where centuries-old architecture stands shoulder-to-shoulder with modern skyscrapers and where every street corner hums with the rhythm of ideas. This isn't just a city. It's a living, breathing force of imagination and transformation. It's the place I now call home. And it's where a unique kind of creative energy comes alive—fuelled by diversity, shaped by technology, and driven by the relentless pursuit of innovation.

You see, London is more than a cultural capital. It's the pulse of what I've come to call the "creative corridor"—a global space where creativity and strategy collide to shape the future of marketing. Here, art doesn't just decorate walls; it powers brands. Here, technology doesn't just automate

If you've ever worked in this world—or even dreamt of it—you know it changes you. It changed me.

My own journey began far from these cobbled streets in India, with the curious mind of a computer science student and a heart that beat for stories. Over time and miles, I found myself drawn not just to storytelling but to strategy—to the way stories could move people, build communities, and drive business in profound ways. And somewhere along the path, I realised that creativity wasn't just a nice-to-have; it was the very foundation of success in this fast-paced, ever-evolving global marketplace.

That's what this book is about. It's not just pages filled with theories or checklists—it's part memoir, part guide, and fully a tribute to the incredible world we, as creatives and marketers, are helping to shape. It's a personal and professional reflection on what it means to live and work inside the creative corridor—where borders blur and ideas soar. Innovation is born not in isolation but in connection.

From those first stumbles in content writing and PR to the steep learning curves in global marketing and strategic branding, I've walked the path many of you may be just beginning—or maybe deep into already. I've made mistakes. I've learned. I've grown. And through it all, I've come to understand one truth: creativity is not the domain of a chosen few. It is the birthright of anyone who dares to think differently, speak boldly, and create with purpose.

So, whether you're a marketer looking to stay ahead of the curve, an entrepreneur navigating global expansion, or a creative soul wondering how to turn passion into impact—this book is for you. It offers insights, lessons, and stories that I hope will not just inform but inspire. Because the future belongs to those who can think creatively, act strategically, and connect authentically.

Welcome to *The Creative Corridor*. I'm honoured to have you here.
Let's begin.

Table of Contents

Chapter 1

The Creative Corridor – A Personal Journey from Computer Science into Marketing

There's something profoundly magical about looking back on your life and realising how all the seemingly random decisions and events fit together to bring you exactly where you are supposed to be. It's almost as if the universe has its own way of guiding us, even when we don't see the path clearly at first. When I look back on the early stages of my journey, I can hardly believe how far I've come. My initial steps into the world of computer science were so far removed from anything related to creativity or marketing that it feels almost surreal now to think about it.

At the time, marketing wasn't even a blip on my radar. My days were consumed by coding, algorithms, and system architectures—worlds made up of logic, numbers, and precise, structured thinking. Every line of code was a puzzle, every algorithm a new challenge to solve. It was all about logic and order, and creativity, as we typically think of it, felt like something entirely out of reach—something reserved for artists and dreamers, not for someone like me, immersed in the rigid world of computers.

But somewhere along the way, something shifted. The more I immersed myself in technology and business, the more I began to see how creativity could be woven into even the most technical

fields. I started to understand that creativity wasn't just about designing beautiful things or telling stories—it was about finding new ways to solve problems, connect with people, and create something that resonated on a deeper level. Slowly but surely, my journey started to take an unexpected turn.

And now, here I am, a storyteller who thrives on strategy and an advocate for the power of marketing to inspire change to move hearts and minds. What started as a deep, methodical dive into computer

1

science has, through a series of serendipitous events and realisations, led me to this place—a place where I see creativity, marketing, and business as a powerful force to connect with others and leave a lasting impact.

Looking back, it feels like I've always been heading in this direction, even when I couldn't see it. All the choices I made, all the skills I developed, all the moments of doubt and self-discovery—they were all leading me here. And I believe that sometimes, when we take a step back, we can see just how everything in our lives, no matter how disconnected it may seem at the time, can come together in the most unexpected and beautiful ways.

So, how did I get here?

How My Tech Background Shaped My Marketing Mindset

In the early days, my routine revolved around solving binary puzzles and debugging endless lines of code. I was trained to think in black and white, to look for clear outcomes and optimise for efficiency. But even within those seemingly rigid boundaries, I found something beautiful — the joy of solving problems and creating something from nothing. That, as I later discovered, wasn't so different from what marketers do.

As I moved into the world of marketing, I realised just how much my technical background had prepared me for it — though not in the ways I'd initially imagined.

Let me be honest: when I first started learning about branding, storytelling, and customer engagement, it felt foreign. I wasn't used to relying on emotion, intuition, or psychology. But here's the twist — marketing, in today's world, is no longer about fluffy slogans or vague instincts. It's about **insights**, **data**, and **strategy**. It's about combining creativity with precision. And that's exactly where my tech training came in.

Programming taught me discipline. It taught me how to break complex problems into smaller parts, test ideas, and improve iteratively. That same mindset helped me understand user journeys, craft marketing funnels, and decode customer behaviour. While others might have relied purely on gut instinct, I had data on my side — not to replace creativity, but to **empower it**.

For instance, in my first role in content marketing, I wasn't just writing articles. I was tracking how many people clicked, how long they stayed, and where they dropped off. I was asking: *Why did this piece work and that one didn't?* That analytical approach, born from my computer science days, helped me optimise content, design better campaigns, and speak the language of both creatives and tech teams.

And let's not forget the tools. Marketing automation, CRM systems, data dashboards — I embraced them all with confidence, understanding not just how to use them but *why* they worked. My familiarity with technology allowed me to move faster, make better decisions, and bridge gaps between departments that often struggle to collaborate.

Over time, I stopped seeing technology and creativity as opposites. Instead, I saw them as partners — two sides of the same coin. With the right mindset, data can spark ideas. Algorithms can uncover human truths. And code? It can tell stories, too.

I came to believe that creativity isn't always about painting outside the lines. Sometimes, it's about building new frames altogether — frames that only someone who understands both logic and emotion can construct.

So yes, my journey started in computer science. But it led me to something far more colourful, emotional, and alive. And if there's one thing I've learned, it's that no knowledge is ever wasted — especially when you're walking your own unique path through the creative corridor.

The Transition from Coding to Content Creation

You know, on paper, moving from coding to content creation sounds like a complete shift — like trading a black-and-white world for one bursting with colour. One is rooted in logic, the other in emotion.

But the funny thing is, once I made that leap, I realised the two weren't as different as they seemed.

I still remember the moment I first dipped my toes into content writing. I came from a background in system architecture and clean, structured code. I'd spent years solving technical problems — building programs, fixing bugs, running simulations. Then, suddenly, I found myself staring at a blank document, wondering how to communicate a brand's message to its audience. And to be completely honest — it was terrifying. But it was also thrilling.

What pulled me toward this new path was curiosity. I'd become fascinated with how brands spoke to people — how they made them feel seen, understood and inspired. I started noticing ads that made me laugh, stories that tugged at something deeper. I wanted to be part of that magic.

At first, it felt like I'd walked into a different universe. But as I settled into the work, I began to notice something familiar. Just like with coding, content creation is about solving problems. It was about understanding what people needed — not from software this time, but from a story, a headline, or a call to action — and delivering it with precision.

And here's a little secret I discovered along the way: words are powerful. Just as lines of code can build something from nothing, the right words can move hearts, change minds, and inspire action. I found myself falling in love with the process

— crafting messages, understanding audiences, and playing with tone and voice until it felt *just right*.

But make no mistake — this wasn't just about creativity floating freely in the air. My background in coding helped me bring a structured mindset to the process. I didn't just write and hope for the best — I tested, measured, refined. I looked at engagement data, bounce rates, and heat maps. I wanted to know: *What's working?*

What isn't? Much like debugging, content writing became a process of iteration and constant improvement.

There were times I felt completely out of my depth. Times when I doubted whether I had any right to call myself a "creative." But slowly, I learned that creativity isn't about being whimsical or spontaneous all the time. It's about being intentional. It's about listening — really listening — to what people need and finding a way to respond beautifully and effectively.

That's when it all clicked for me. Marketing isn't a fight between logic and emotion

— it's a dance between them. The best campaigns, the most powerful pieces of content, don't just *feel* right. They work because they're backed by data, grounded in insight, and fuelled by empathy.

Leveraging Analytical Skills in Creative Industries

As I found my footing in marketing, something unexpected happened — I started to realise that my analytical skills, the ones I thought I'd left behind in the world of coding, were actually my secret weapon.

Let's face it — creativity alone doesn't cut it anymore, not in today's digital world. If you're not using data, you're flying blind. And for someone like me, who'd spent years analysing patterns, building logic trees, and solving complex technical problems, this was familiar terrain.

I began to see every piece of content, every campaign, and every social media post as part of a bigger system. A living, breathing algorithm of human behaviour. I'd look at website traffic like a map. Click-through rates were signals. Bounce rates? Warnings. Every metric told a story, and it was my job to read it.

The same skills I once used to debug lines of code, I now use to troubleshoot underperforming content. What's missing? Why isn't this landing? How can I improve it? That analytical lens helped me iterate faster and with more confidence.

And then there was SEO — Search Engine Optimisation — the great invisible force behind so much of our digital world. To me, understanding search engine algorithms felt oddly familiar. I approached them the same way I would an unfamiliar codebase: learning the logic, identifying the patterns, and figuring out how to work within (and sometimes around) the rules.

Of course, I wasn't just doing this for clicks. It wasn't about gaming the system. It was about making sure the right people found the right content — content that could genuinely help them, inform them, or make them feel understood. That's what marketing is about, after all. Not manipulation, but connection.

And here's what's truly exciting: when creativity and data come together, the possibilities explode. Imagine this — you write two versions of an ad, A/B test them and discover that Version B performs 40% better. Why? Was it the headline? The tone? The colour of the button? You dive into the data, you learn, and the next campaign is even stronger.

That kind of feedback loop — create, test, learn, adapt — is what makes modern marketing so powerful. And it's why analytical thinkers like me have a real edge in the creative world.

Looking back, my journey from computer science to marketing wasn't just a career change — it was a personal evolution. I didn't abandon logic for creativity. I discovered a way to fuse them. In doing so, I found a space where I could be both analytical and imaginative, both precise and expressive.

So, if you're someone with a "technical" background wondering if there's room for you in the creative world, let me tell you: there absolutely is. The future of marketing belongs to those who can think across disciplines, who can balance intuition with insight, and who aren't afraid to mix a little code with their content.

Because in the end, it's all about solving problems — and telling stories that matter.

Navigating Cross-Cultural Challenges

In today's connected world, the ability to navigate cultural differences isn't just a skill—it's a lifeline, especially in a field like marketing, where understanding human emotions and behaviours across borders is everything. My journey—from the bustling, vibrant streets of India, where I first stepped into the professional world, to the structured and creatively rich environment of the UK—has been nothing short of transformative. And it's these experiences that have shaped not only my outlook as a marketer but also my growth as a person.

I want to take you with me through the moments that tested me, taught me, and ultimately transformed my approach to creativity and strategy. Because in the end, it's not just about marketing products—it's about connecting with people. This section dives deep into the cultural shifts I experienced, the bridges I had to build between tradition and innovation, and how stepping out of my comfort zone opened up a whole new world of understanding.

Cultural Differences in the UK and India

India and the UK—two countries with rich histories and layered cultures—couldn't be more different in how they see the world, yet both have taught me so much about the human side of marketing.

Growing up and working in India, I was immersed in a culture where community and family take centre stage. Everything from decision-making to daily routines is often influenced by collective values. In marketing, this translates to stories that tug at the heartstrings—campaigns rich in emotion, grounded in tradition, and centred around family, unity, and heritage. Think of a Diwali campaign where lights and laughter bring generations together—it's not just a sales pitch; it's a celebration of connection.

Then came the UK—a place that embraces independence, personal achievement, and self-expression. Here, marketing feels like a mirror reflecting the individual's voice. Campaigns celebrate uniqueness, promote bold self-expression, and champion personal success. It was a cultural shift I didn't just witness—I lived it. And with that came the realisation that a campaign steeped in emotion and familial warmth, which would shine in India, might seem overly sentimental in the UK. Likewise, the witty sarcasm in a British ad might miss the mark in an Indian context, where humour is more expressive and rooted in shared experiences.

Navigating these contrasts wasn't easy. I remember pitching an emotionally driven campaign during my early days in the UK—it had worked wonders in India. But the response here? "Too melodramatic," someone said. That moment stung. But it was also the moment I truly understood that effective marketing starts with listening—really listening—to the culture.

That's when I began to craft a culturally adaptive lens for every campaign. I learned to tune into the emotional rhythms of each audience—to pick up on what moves them, excites them, or even annoys them. Whether it's the Indian respect for elders or the British love for independence, understanding these subtle cues became my secret weapon. It was no longer about simply telling stories—it was about telling the *right* story in the *right* voice to the *right* people.

How Global Perspectives Enhance Marketing Strategy

Living and working across cultures gifted me with a superpower I never expected: perspective. And in marketing, that's pure gold.

When you step out of one culture and into another, your lens widens. You start to notice patterns, behaviours, and even silences. In the UK, my MBA journey exposed me to global trends—how digital innovation is reshaping everything, how sustainability is becoming more than just a buzzword, and how inclusivity is no longer a 'nice-to-have' but a necessity. Suddenly, I wasn't just thinking like a marketer from India or adapting to the UK—I was thinking globally.

Having a global perspective forces you to ask better questions: *Who are we talking to? What matters to them? How do we speak their language—not just linguistically, but emotionally?* That's where real strategy begins.

And with that came a shift in how I approached every project. For instance, take the trend of hyper-personalisation. In the UK, where consumers value independence and tech-savvy solutions, AI-driven personalisation is embraced with open arms. In India, however, people might hesitate—preferring human interaction and emotional trust over automated convenience. These insights aren't just academic—they're real, grounded, and necessary when crafting campaigns that work across borders.

I've come to love the complexity that global marketing brings. It's like solving a giant, ever-changing puzzle—where every piece represents a different culture, value, or expectation. And the joy comes when you find that perfect fit—when a campaign clicks because it's not just clever or creative but deeply *human*.

Diversity, I've realised, isn't just about demographics. It's a creative advantage. It opens up new ways of thinking, challenges assumptions, and encourages marketers like me to step beyond our comfort zones. Global perspectives help us build not only better strategies but better stories—ones that resonate because they reflect the real, diverse world we live in.

Adapting to the UK's Creative Environment

Moving to the UK wasn't just a change of address—it was a change of mindset.

The creative industry here is fast, bold, and unafraid to push boundaries. It's a space where ideas are currency, and standing still is simply not an option. I quickly realised that what worked in India—a more methodical, process-driven approach— wasn't enough here. The UK thrives on innovation, and to keep up, I had to unlearn and relearn. Fast.

I remember my first pitch meeting here. My slides were neat, my data solid—but something was missing. "Where's the spark?" someone asked. That question haunted me for weeks. Until it didn't. Soon, I found my rhythm in this creative chaos.

In this environment, success comes to those who dare to think differently. I began to immerse myself in digital tools, explore cutting-edge platforms, and embrace storytelling formats that were more dynamic and immersive. Creativity here isn't a department—it's the lifeblood of every campaign.

Another adjustment was the way people communicate. In the UK, clarity and directness are valued. Feedback is honest, sometimes brutally so—but always aimed at making things better. It was different from the more nuanced, respectful tone I was used to in India, where hierarchy often guides interactions. Learning to speak up to assert ideas confidently was a growth curve—but one I'm grateful for. It helped me find my voice, both creatively and professionally.

Understanding the UK audience also meant shifting how I built brand narratives. Here, individuality is king. Campaigns that empower the consumer that tell *their* story tend to resonate most. I had to recalibrate—not abandon the emotional storytelling I'd honed in India, but adapt it to a culture that values self-discovery and personal identity.

And that adaptation has been incredibly empowering. It's stretched my imagination, sharpened my instincts, and, most importantly, reminded me that creativity knows no borders—it just needs the right context.

Navigating cross-cultural challenges has been one of the most defining aspects of my career. It's taught me to slow down and listen, to observe without judgment, and to respect what makes each culture beautifully unique. The lessons I've learned from both India and the UK—from their contrasts, their contradictions, and their shared humanity—have shaped the marketer I am today.

In a world where brands are expected to be not just seen but *felt*, having the ability to read between cultural lines is a superpower every marketer should strive for. My journey has shown me that when we bring creativity and cultural awareness together, we don't just market better—we connect deeper.

And in the end, isn't that what we're all trying to do?

Lessons from My Journey

Throughout my career, I've had my fair share of ups, downs, and unexpected turns—each one leaving a mark on how I think, work, and create. The path I followed wasn't a straight line. In fact, it was anything but. I started out in computer science, surrounded by logic, code, and structure. And yet, here I am—advocating for creative innovation in marketing, chasing stories, crafting strategies, and helping brands connect with people on a deeply human level.

The journey has been messy, beautiful, and, at times, terrifying. But every twist came with a lesson. Every risk, every setback, every breakthrough taught me something that has shaped who I am—not just as a professional, but as a person. So, in this section, I want to share some of those lessons with you. Not as checklists or bullet points, but as lived experiences—because if you're carving your own path in the creative industries, I hope they'll offer you something real to hold onto.

Embracing Risk and Change in My Career

One of the most powerful lessons I've learned—possibly *the* most powerful—was to stop clinging to certainty. Like many people, I started my professional life chasing security. My degree in computer science was a safe bet. It made sense. It came with a map. But deep down, something didn't feel right.

I was good at coding. I could solve problems, write clean logic, and think in systems. But there was a part of me that longed for more—more creativity, more connection, more storytelling. The deeper I went into tech, the more I felt like I was wearing someone else's clothes. And eventually, I had to ask myself the hard question: *What do I actually want to wake up and do every day?*

That question changed everything.

Walking away from a defined, stable path was terrifying. I had no

11

formal background in marketing. No textbook had prepared me for what was coming. But I knew, in my gut, that I had to pivot. So, I did. I took a leap of faith and started from scratch—as a content writer at ETTG Data Corporation. It wasn't glamorous. But it was mine.

Those early days were humbling. I was learning on the go, soaking up everything I could. I started noticing how my technical skills—analytical thinking, the ability to see patterns, the structured way of breaking down problems—actually gave me an unexpected advantage. I wasn't just telling stories; I was building bridges between creativity and data. And that combination? It became my superpower.

Of course, there were moments of doubt—moments where I'd lie awake wondering if I'd made a mistake. But risk, I've learned, isn't something to fear. It's a door. Sometimes, it creaks open. Sometimes, you have to kick it down. But behind it lies possibility.

Today, I stand on a foundation built from both worlds—tech and creativity—and that fusion allows me to see problems through multiple lenses. I can dream big, but I can also back it up with logic and structure. That's the kind of edge you get when you embrace change instead of running from it. And if there's one truth I've come to live by, it's this: the most meaningful growth often begins right where comfort ends.

Applying Creativity to Real-World Marketing Challenges

When people hear the word "creativity," they often think of painters, musicians, designers—people who make beautiful things. But I've learned that creativity is much more than that. It's not just an artistic expression; it's a mindset. It's a way of looking at the world and asking, *What if we tried something different?*

At the start of my marketing journey, I thought creativity lived only in content—in the words I wrote, the stories I shaped. But the deeper I went, the more I realised creativity is *everywhere*. It's in the strategy, the analytics, the timing, the audience targeting. It's in the ability to see a problem from a fresh angle and find a solution no one else saw coming.

During my time at Adfactors PR, I was thrown into the deep end. I worked with clients across industries—each with its own voice and its own challenges. I remember one campaign vividly. It was for a health and wellness brand, and I had to figure out how to turn scientific data into something people would actually *want* to read. It wasn't just about simplifying language. It was about telling a story—one that made people feel seen, understood, and empowered.

That's where creativity came in. I had to marry facts with emotion, logic, with empathy. It wasn't easy. But the result? A campaign that didn't just inform people—it connected with them. And that, I realised, was the real job of a marketer.

Later, during my MBA in the UK, the challenge became even more global. I had to think about scalability, cross-cultural appeal, and digital fluency. One project in particular—a digital campaign for a luxury lifestyle brand—pushed me to reimagine how to reach high-net-worth individuals while maintaining a consistent global identity. It wasn't just about luxury; it was about relevance. Every market had its nuances, and our message had to flex without breaking.

And here's the beautiful part: creativity *thrives* when it's paired with data. I started using my computer science background to track trends, analyse behaviour, and predict responses. Suddenly, creativity wasn't just an idea—it was measurable, adaptable, and strategic. It had a purpose.

So, if there's one thing I want you to take away, it's this: creativity isn't magic. It's a tool. One that, when used well, can solve real problems and spark real change. The trick is to look beyond the obvious. To question the default. To experiment, test, and evolve. And to never, ever stop learning.

The Importance of Networking in Creative Industries

I'll admit something: I used to think networking was... awkward. Forced. A little self-serving, even. I assumed that if I just kept my head down and worked hard, opportunities would naturally follow.

I was wrong.

The creative industries are built on relationships. Ideas grow when they're shared. Projects thrive when they're collaborative. And the best opportunities? They often come from the quiet conversations—the coffee chats, the introductions, the spontaneous connections at events you almost didn't attend.

When I moved to the UK, the power of networking hit me in full force. I was in a new environment, surrounded by insanely talented people from all walks of life. Designers, strategists, creatives, entrepreneurs. Each one had a story, a vision, and something to teach me.

At first, I was nervous. Would they take me seriously? Did I belong in those rooms? But slowly, I started to show up—at industry events, workshops, creative mixers. And each time, I walked away with more than just contacts. I walked away with ideas, collaborations, feedback, and friendships.

Networking, I realised, isn't about asking for something. It's about *sharing* something. Your perspective. Your enthusiasm. Your support. And when you give genuinely, it comes back tenfold.

One of the most rewarding parts of building a creative network is the energy it brings. When you're around people who are passionate, curious, and driven, it's contagious. You start to push yourself further. You think bigger. And you stop feeling like you're in this alone.

And here's the truth: some of my proudest projects, biggest leaps, and boldest ideas came from conversations that started with a simple "Hey, I love what you're working on."

So, whether you're just starting out or deep into your career, don't underestimate the power of connection. Creativity doesn't exist in a vacuum—it's a living, breathing force nurtured by people who believe in something greater than themselves. Be one of those people. Find your tribe. And once you do, lift each other up.

The lessons I've gathered from my journey—about risk, creativity, and community—aren't just checkboxes on a resume. They're the heartbeat of everything I do. Choosing to take the road less certain led me to a career I love. Choosing to see creativity as a strategy helped me find my voice in the industry. And choosing to open myself up to people brought me a network that feels like a creative family.

If you're navigating your own path in the creative world, here's what I'll leave you with: be brave enough to pivot, curious enough to create, and kind enough to connect. The rest? It will come.

Chapter 2
The Creative Economy Is Here to Stay
Understanding the Shift

Let's take a moment to pause, shall we? I mean, really pause. Close your eyes for a second, take a deep breath, and just listen. Feel the world around you. Can you sense it? The energy? The movement? Now, take a good look at everything, everything that's unfolding before you. Have you noticed how incredibly different things are today? It's almost as if the world we knew has completely transformed, and we're living in a reality that seems both familiar and foreign at the same time.

Think about it for a second—how we do business, how we connect with one another, how we create, and even how we consume—it's almost unrecognisable compared to just a few decades ago. Our lives are being reshaped in ways we couldn't have imagined before. What we once thought was the "norm" has shifted, and in its place, a whole new way of thinking, working, and living has emerged. And let me tell you, it's exciting, even a little overwhelming at times, isn't it?

So, what's behind this transformation? What's driving it all? What force is reshaping the world we know, altering how we interact, and pushing us into new territories every single day?

Here's the twist—the surprise: it's creativity. Yes, creativity. It's the spark that's igniting change across every industry, every culture, and every corner of our world. It's creativity that's powering the revolution we're witnessing today.

You might be thinking, "Really? Is it that simple?" But think about it for a moment. Creativity isn't just about art or music or innovation in the traditional sense. It's the heartbeat of everything we do. It's in the way we approach problems, the way we communicate, and the way we find new paths where none existed before. In business, creativity is no longer just the responsibility of designers and artists; it's at the core of how we connect with our customers, how we solve problems, how we lead teams, and how we shape the future.

The tools may have changed, and the environment may be different, but the driving force behind it all—the force that has the power to connect people from different corners of the globe, to challenge old ways of thinking, to open up entirely new industries—is creativity. And the more we embrace it, the more we allow it to flow freely, the more we can build, connect, and innovate in ways we never thought possible.

So, I ask you: Are you ready to step into this new reality? Are you ready to harness the power of creativity and use it to shape the world around you? Because this is just the beginning, and the creative revolution is only getting started.

Yes, creativity. That very thing we often think of as "art" or "design" or maybe even something abstract. In truth, creativity is no longer confined to just the artists or the dreamers. It's the backbone of every industry, the force that propels businesses forward, helping them stand out in a world where everything feels overcrowded. The rise of the **creative economy** isn't just some fleeting trend. It's a **profound** shift— a wave that's washing over every corner of our professional and personal lives. And it's not just here to stay; it's **redesigning** what success looks like across industries.

But why does this matter so much? Why should we pay attention to this creative revolution?

Well, the answer is simple. In the world of marketing, for example, the old ways of doing things—the tried-and-true strategies—are quickly becoming obsolete. It's not enough to just follow the rules anymore. Today, **innovation** is the name of the game. It's about pushing boundaries, trying things that haven't been done before, and taking **risks** to create something that feels fresh, original, and deeply **human**.

In this section, I want to take you on a journey through what this shift actually looks like. I want to show you how marketing has moved from rigid structures and predictable outcomes to a world that's **bold**, **inventive**, and often a little messy— but in the best way possible. We're in an age where brands are no longer just selling products—they're telling stories, creating experiences, and building connections that matter on a personal level. And that's because creativity is no longer a "nice-to-have." It's become the driving force behind every meaningful, successful venture.

So, let's dive into it together. I'll walk you through the evolution of the creative economy, what it means for you, and why embracing creativity is the key to unlocking the future of marketing—and beyond.

The Rise of the Creative Economy

For much of the 20th century, business built on a fairly straightforward formula: produce at scale, keep costs low, and push products out to the masses. You probably remember those old-school ads—catchy jingles on TV, big billboards, or glossy magazine spreads. Back then, consumers were seen as passive audiences, quietly absorbing messages delivered to them through traditional media.

But everything changed with the dawn of the 21st century.

The internet arrived, digital tools exploded, and suddenly—everything was different. We entered an era where consumers weren't just listening anymore; they were speaking, interacting, shaping brands, and creating their own narratives. The creative economy was born at this moment. What used to be a one-way street became a dynamic two-way exchange, and those who understood this early on started reaping the rewards.

I like to think of the creative economy as more than just a business model—it's a mindset. It's where ideas, culture, stories, and human experiences become valuable assets. Think about how content marketing has taken over or how social media influencers now drive purchasing decisions. This isn't just marketing—it's culture in motion. Brands like Apple, Spotify, and Nike have embraced this shift wholeheartedly, building identities that go far beyond their products.

But here's something even more exciting: creativity isn't boxed into one corner of the market. It's in architecture, automotive design, fashion, technology, and even in sectors you wouldn't immediately think of. It's no wonder that, in countries like the UK, the creative industries now contribute over £100 billion to the economy. That's not just a number—it's a reflection of how deeply creativity has woven itself into our economic fabric.

Why Creativity Drives Modern Business

Now, let's talk about what this really means for business.

Creativity today isn't just about pretty packaging or catchy slogans. It's about solving real problems, making emotional connections, and offering something truly different in a sea of sameness. In a world where consumers are constantly bombarded with messages, creativity is what makes people pause, pay attention, and, most importantly—care.

At its core, creativity is fuel for innovation. It's how businesses stay ahead, introducing new products and experiences that actually matter. It's also how they stay human. People don't just want a product; they want a story, a connection, a reason to believe.

Nike's "Just Do It" campaign is a perfect example. It's not just a slogan—it's a rallying cry that taps into ambition, resilience, and emotion. That campaign transformed Nike from a shoe company into a source of inspiration for millions. And all of it was powered by creative thinking.

But creativity isn't just about inspiring people—it's about resilience, too. It's about the ability to pivot when things change. Remember Kodak? Once a giant in the photography industry, it failed to innovate creatively when digital photography emerged. Compare that to companies like Netflix or Amazon, which continually reimagine their offerings, driven by both data and imagination. That's the difference creative thinking makes.

And let's not forget how creativity drives value—real, measurable value. Today, a brand's identity, its emotional impact, and the stories it tells can be worth billions. Apple's brand, for example, isn't just a logo—it's a lifestyle. That's the power of creativity in action.

Moving from Traditional Marketing to Creative Innovation

The way we communicate with audiences has changed so much. Back in the day, marketing was all about sending messages out and hoping they stuck. You'd run an ad, mail a brochure, or maybe do a product demo. But that world has shifted, and thank goodness for that.

Today's consumers want more—they want to engage, interact, and even co-create. They want to be part of the story. And that's where creative innovation steps in.

Think about content marketing. Instead of shouting, it speaks. Instead of selling, it serves. Companies now share valuable, helpful, and entertaining content—blog posts, videos, even TikToks—that build trust and connection over time. It's more than a strategy—it's a relationship.

Then there's experiential marketing. This is where brands step off the screen and into real life. Imagine Red Bull's extreme sports events or pop-up brand experiences that make people stop in their tracks. Marketing becomes something you *feel*, not just something you see.

But being creative doesn't mean being random. The smartest marketers today combine creativity with data. Using analytics, behavioural insights, and real-time feedback, they craft personalised experiences that truly resonate. Creativity is backed by intelligence—that's the secret sauce.

And something I've learned along the way is that this shift also requires collaboration. Creatives, technologists, strategists, data analysts—they all need to work together. When different minds come together, magic happens. Walls between departments fall, and suddenly, new ideas flourish.

This creative shift we're talking about? It's not just a passing trend, something we can dip our toes into and ride for a while. No, my friend, this is the new tide we're all swimming in. We're immersed in it. We can't ignore it, and we certainly can't wait for it to pass. Creativity has become more than a nice addition to what we do—it's now a must-have. It's the spark that ignites everything we do. It's what will make us stand out in a sea of competition. It's what will help us not just survive but truly thrive.

Now, I know this might feel overwhelming. Whether you're a business owner, a marketer, or simply someone trying to make sense of the whirlwind world around you, I want you to know this: You're not alone. We are all in this together. The world is shifting, and yes, it's a bit daunting, but it's also full of possibilities. The truth is the future belongs to those who are bold enough to be different. To those who dare to tell new stories that haven't been told yet. To those who are brave enough to reinvent themselves and their businesses, no matter how scary that may seem.

The creative economy isn't just a buzzword or some vague idea we're all supposed to nod along to. It's here. Right now. And it's not going anywhere. It's evolving, it's growing, and if we're willing to embrace it, we will evolve and grow with it. But here's the catch: we can't wait for change to happen to us. We have to be the ones to lead it. We have to step forward with confidence and vision, ready to steer the ship, not just follow the current.

Because, at the end of the day, creativity is what connects us. It's the thread that ties us together as humans. It's the emotion behind every brand story, every marketing campaign, and every product that captures our imagination. It's the thing that moves us, that inspires us, and that challenges us to dream bigger. Creativity is the fuel that will carry us forward in this exciting, unpredictable, and beautifully human business landscape we find ourselves.

So, as we stand on the edge of this massive shift, I ask you to stop and think for a moment: How will you respond? Will you resist the tide, or will you dive in, ready to create and lead with everything you've got?

Let's choose to lead. Let's embrace this change because the future is ours to shape, and creativity is the key to unlocking it.

Creativity as the New Currency

Let's face it—something big is happening in the world of business. You can feel it, right? The way we connect with brands, make decisions, even form opinions about companies... it's all changing. And at the heart of this transformation is one very powerful force: *creativity*.

The creative economy has completely redefined how businesses think about growth, engagement, and their place in people's lives. In today's hyper-connected, fast-moving world, creativity is no longer a 'nice-to-have'—it's become the new currency. A kind of emotional and intellectual capital that brands are using to connect deeply with customers, stand out in an ocean of sameness, and build something that lasts.

In this section, I want to walk you through why creativity matters more than ever. We'll explore how it's become one of the most valuable assets in today's digital-first business landscape, how it fuels brand loyalty, and why it's now one of the biggest differentiators between those who thrive—and those who fade into the background.

The Value of Creativity in the Digital Age

If you've been in business—or just been observing it—you already know that things don't work the way they used to. Gone are the days when a catchy jingle or a flashy print ad was enough to win over your audience. Today's consumers are *everywhere*, and they're paying attention to *everything*.

In the past, the strategy was pretty straightforward: create a message, push it out through mass media, and hope it sticks. But now? People have *choices*. They've got the entire world in their pockets, and that means your message—no matter how well-crafted—has to *compete* with thousands of others. It's exhausting, isn't it?

That's why creativity is so critical in this digital age. It's what helps your message break through the noise. It's what makes someone stop scrolling, lean in, and think, *"Huh... this feels different."* Whether it's a beautifully shot video, a quirky meme that hits just right, or a story that tugs at the heartstrings—creativity invites connection.

But here's the thing—creativity isn't just about being visually impressive or coming up with a clever tagline. It's also about *relevance*. By combining creativity with tools like AI, analytics, and big data, businesses can create messages that don't just speak *to* people—they speak *with* them. It's that balance—between logic and emotion, art and science—that creates real impact.

Brand Loyalty and Emotional Connection

Now, let me ask you something: when was the last time a brand truly *moved* you?

In today's market, loyalty isn't built on price tags or product specs alone. People want more. They want to feel something. They want to see themselves reflected in a brand's story—to know that a company *gets* them. And that's where creativity becomes absolutely magical.

It's the emotional layer that turns a product into a passion. It's what transforms a brand from just another logo into something personal, something meaningful.

Think back to Coca-Cola's "Share a Coke" campaign. Seeing your name—or a friend's—on a bottle? It felt intimate, didn't it? Suddenly, a soft drink wasn't just a refreshment. It was a moment. A memory. A smile was shared between people. That's creativity at work—building not just recognition but *relationships*.

Nike, too, has mastered this. "Just Do It" is more than a slogan—it's a *mantra*. It's a call to action for anyone who's ever faced self-doubt, a whisper in your ear saying, *"You've got this."* Through storytelling, visual narrative, and bold creative choices, Nike makes people *feel* empowered—and that feeling sticks.

When you build an emotional connection, you're not just earning a one-time sale. You're earning *trust*. You're earning a place in someone's life. And in a world of infinite options and easy comparison shopping, that kind of loyalty is priceless.

Creativity as a Market Differentiator

Let's be real—it's *loud* out there. Every brand is screaming for attention, throwing their messages into the void, hoping something will stick. But here's the truth: if you blend in, you risk fading away completely. Think about it—if your brand feels like just another copy-paste version of everyone else, why would people choose you? Why would they remember you?

That's where creativity comes in. Creativity is your sharpest edge. It's your ticket to standing out in the crowd. It's what makes people sit up and take notice. It's the reason why someone will talk about your brand, root for it, and come back for more.

Take Apple, for instance. It's not just about the technology they make—it's about the entire experience. The way the product feels in your hands, the sleek packaging, the simplicity of the interface, even the way the store is laid out—everything is designed with care, with intention, with style. It's a world that Apple has built, and we're all invited in. They don't just sell gadgets; they sell a lifestyle, an experience. That's the magic of creativity—it's not just about what you offer but about how you make someone *feel.*

And then there's Tesla—oh, Tesla. They didn't just create a car. They redefined what a car could be. But even more than that, they're disrupting entire mindsets. When you think of Tesla, you don't just think of electric vehicles. You think of innovation, sustainability, and a future that's cleaner and brighter. Creativity here doesn't just change a product—it transforms how we see the world. And that's powerful.

Even in industries where products seem almost interchangeable—like food, for example—creativity makes a huge difference. Look at Ben & Jerry's. It's not just ice cream; it's a personality in a pint. They've taken something simple and made it *fun, cheeky,* and *conscious.* They've built a brand that feels like a friend you can trust. Or Innocent Drinks—smoothies that don't just hydrate but *speak* to you. They make you feel good about what you're drinking, about the choices you're making. That's the power of creativity: it doesn't just say, "Here's what we offer." It says, "Here's who we are—and here's how we make your life better."

But here's the thing: creativity isn't just about the flashy ads or the cool product design. It's in the little things, too. The things you might not notice at first. Like customer service. Like the user experience. That's where companies like Amazon and Zappos shine. They didn't become giants by accident. They thought about what it feels like to shop—what it feels like to *be* a customer—and they reimagined that entire experience. They made it easier, more personal, more human. And that kind of creativity? It sticks. It builds trust. It keeps people coming back for more, time and time again.

So, remember this: creativity isn't just about standing out—it's about connecting, about building relationships that last. When you bring creativity to the table, you're not just offering a product or service. You're offering an experience, a story, a part of yourself. And that's what people will remember. That's what will make them choose you.

Creativity as the Key to Sustainable Business Success

So, what's the big takeaway here?

Let's pause for a moment and get real. Creativity isn't just a nice-to-have. It's not some fluffy add-on, not a final touch that you toss on top of your business strategy when you're feeling fancy. No. Creativity is the *core*. It's the engine that drives progress, that builds connections, that fuels growth. It's the human heartbeat that pulses through the very soul of a brand.

If there's one thing I want you to remember, one truth that I hope sticks with you, it's this: in the world we're living in today—fast-paced, constantly changing, and emotionally charged—creativity is not just a tool. It's *your lifeline*. It's what will keep you afloat when the waters get rough. It's the one thing that will keep your brand not just surviving but thriving in a world that doesn't stop spinning.

Here's the thing: we're all navigating a world that demands more from us every day. It's a world where attention spans are shrinking, where customers are overwhelmed by choices, and where change is the only constant. And in a world like that, what sets the winners apart from the rest isn't just a great product or a slick marketing campaign—it's creativity. Creativity is what makes you stand out when everyone else is blending in. It's what allows you to speak to people on a deeper level, to connect in a way that feels *real, authentic,* and *human.*

The brands that truly embrace creativity are the ones that will stand the test of time. They won't just compete for space—they'll *lead.* They'll shape the future of their industries. Think about the companies that have made an impact over the years. They didn't do it by playing it safe. They did it by taking risks, by thinking differently, and by daring to be creative. They're the brands that stay relevant, that inspire us, that *live* in our hearts.

And if you're serious about building something that lasts—something that resonates not just today but for years to come—then creativity has to be at the centre of everything you do. It's the most valuable currency you can invest in. It's the thing that will help you weather any storm, that will keep you moving forward, and that will allow you to build a legacy.

So, let creativity be the force that drives you. Let it be the foundation you build on. Because when you invest in creativity, you're investing in something that lasts. And that's how you build a business that not only survives the ever-changing tides but thrives in them.

Shaping the Future of Marketing

The world of marketing is changing faster than ever before — and right at the heart of that change is creativity. As we step into an increasingly complex digital age, creativity isn't just another piece of the puzzle; it's the key to unlocking the future of marketing.

Let me take you through why this matters.

From bold innovations to market-shaking disruptions, creativity is driving us forward. It's reshaping how consumers behave and opening doors to new, previously unimagined opportunities. In this section, I want to explore with you how creativity fuels innovation, triggers disruption, and intersects with technology to shape the future of how we tell stories, build brands, and connect with people like never before.

Creativity's Role in Innovation and Disruption

Creativity and innovation — they've always been close companions. But today, creativity does more than inspire; it disrupts. It turns industries on their heads, rewrites market rules, and reshapes what customers expect.

Disruption, at its core, is about daring to be different. It's about saying, "We don't have to do it the way it's always been done." And honestly, that takes guts — and a lot of creative thinking. Businesses that truly break away from the norm do so by developing fresh products, unique services, and unforgettable experiences that make people stop and take notice.

In marketing, innovation isn't limited to shiny new tech or products. It's about revolutionising the way businesses connect with people — with you and me. The most disruptive brands out there! They don't just sell; they immerse, surprise, and move us. And at the heart of that impact is creativity — pure, powerful, boundary-pushing creativity.

Take Airbnb, for instance. It didn't just offer a new way to book a room. It completely reimagined what travel could feel like — more personal, more authentic. By thinking beyond the hotel experience and inviting everyday people to open their homes, Airbnb created something truly magical: a sense of belonging. That shift wasn't just clever; it was deeply human. And it was made possible by creative thinking, blending tech with empathy in a way that made all the difference.

Amazon, too, is a masterclass in creative disruption. Whether it's one-click purchases, Prime benefits, or cashier-less Amazon Go stores, the company keeps asking, "How can we make life easier?" And through constant innovation, it's redefined convenience and changed how the world shops. Creativity, in Amazon's case, is like a sixth sense — always alert to how people live and what they need next.

Now, think about Nike. This brand doesn't just make shoes — it tells stories, ignites inspiration, and brings entire communities together. Its campaigns are more than ads; they're powerful messages of perseverance, identity, and drive. Nike shows us how creativity and innovation, when woven together, can transcend products and touch something deeper in the human spirit.

Disruptive strategies begin with listening — really listening — to what people want, what they struggle with, and what they dream of. By spotting unmet needs or overlooked voices, businesses can use creativity not just to solve problems but to spark movements. That's the soul of innovation in marketing today.

Future Trends in Creative Marketing

Let's be honest — keeping up with the future of marketing can feel overwhelming. But it's also exciting. Creativity, when combined with evolving trends and tech, creates a playground of possibilities for brands and consumers alike.

One major trend you've probably noticed is personalisation. Today, we don't just want brands to know our names; we want them to know us — what we like, what we care about, and how we live. With AI, big data, and machine learning, brands now have the tools to create content and experiences that speak directly to us as individuals.

And it's not just a gimmick. Personalisation makes people feel seen and valued. Take Spotify's "Discover Weekly" — a brilliant example of data meeting heart.

It's not just a playlist; it's a thoughtful gesture that says, "Hey, we get you." Amazon and Netflix have also nailed this — suggesting exactly what we might enjoy next based on who we are.

Then there's the rise of immersive technologies — AR and VR.

These aren't just futuristic toys. They're opening up new ways for us to engage. Picture this: you're decorating your living room and use an app to see exactly how a new sofa fits your space. That's what IKEA offers with AR. Or imagine trying on makeup virtually, like you can with Sephora's "Virtual Artist." These tools bring joy, convenience, and imagination to the shopping experience.

Another wave we can't ignore is the push toward sustainability and purpose. Today's consumers — especially the younger crowd — care deeply about the planet and social justice. They want to support brands that care, too. So, when a brand creatively showcases its commitment to causes that matter, it's not just smart

— it's necessary. It builds trust, loyalty, and, most importantly, connection.

And let's not forget influencers. They've become the trusted voices in a noisy digital world. Instead of polished ads, people now turn to relatable content from creators they follow and admire. It's why creative marketing now often means collaborating with influencers who can tell a brand's story in a more human, honest way.

All these trends — from AI to AR, from sustainability to influencers — show us one thing: creativity in marketing isn't static. It's fluid, alive, and always evolving.

The Intersection of Technology and Creativity

Here's where things get even more exciting — where creativity and technology meet and spark something extraordinary.

Technology is no longer separate from creativity. It's the fuel that makes creative ideas scalable, smarter, and more impactful. Thanks to powerful tools, marketers can now understand consumer behaviour in real time and tailor campaigns to fit those insights. But — and this is important — data alone doesn't move hearts. That's where creativity steps in, transforming cold numbers into stories, visuals, and moments that resonate.

Think of social media. Platforms like Instagram, TikTok, and YouTube aren't just channels — they're canvases. And with the right blend of creativity and tech, they allow brands to be playful, vulnerable, artistic, and real. Whether it's a short reel, a viral challenge, or an influencer-led tutorial, social media gives us new ways to connect and share in ways that feel human.

And what about automation? Chatbots, recommendation engines, and virtual assistants are everywhere now. But here's the twist: it's creativity that makes them memorable. A chatbot with a personality — one that's funny, helpful, and maybe even a little quirky — can turn a mundane exchange into a delightful experience. It's proof that even the most high-tech tools need a human touch.

In this new era, marketers aren't choosing between tech and creativity. They're combining them to build richer, more meaningful interactions — ones that not only serve but also surprise and delight.

Embracing the Future of Creative Marketing

So, where does all of this leave us?

Right here. At this very moment. At a thrilling, exhilarating crossroads. Can you feel it? That energy in the air, the palpable sense that something big is happening. We're standing at the edge of something new, something exciting. A place where creativity is no longer just a nice-to-have or a buzzword. No, it's essential. It's the lifeblood of everything we do, of everything that's about to unfold in the world of marketing.

The future of marketing, my friends, will belong to those who aren't afraid to be different. To those who are willing to step out of the comfortable, predictable paths and embrace the unknown with curiosity. Those who are ready to face change head-on and see the possibilities, not the obstacles. The future will belong to those who dare to innovate, who don't just look at trends but dive into them with an open mind, seeing not just what's popular now but what could shape the world tomorrow.

And here's the best part: technology, as powerful as it is, isn't here to replace humanity. No, it's here to enhance it. To elevate our creativity, to amplify our connection, and to give us the tools to tell stories in ways we never dreamed possible. It's not about replacing the human touch; it's about using technology as an ally in our journey to create deeper, more meaningful connections with the people we serve.

As we continue to navigate this fast-evolving landscape together, let's remember something crucial: creative marketing isn't about having all the answers. It's about asking better questions. It's about staying curious, always questioning what we think we know, and finding new, bold ways to connect with others. Creativity thrives in the unknown, in the unexplored, in the spaces where the conventional doesn't quite fit.

And as we step into this vibrant future — a future where imagination and innovation go hand in hand — know this: the creative economy is not a passing trend. It's not something that's going to fade away or be replaced by the next big thing. It's here to stay. It's our new reality. And those of us who are willing to embrace it, to nurture it, to live and breathe it every day? Well, we're not just shaping marketing. We're shaping the world itself.

So, what are you waiting for? Let's embrace this future together.

Chapter 3
Building Brands Without Borders

The Need for Global Marketing Strategies

In today's hyperconnected, digital-first world, the idea of building a brand solely within one geographic region feels not only limiting—it's, quite frankly, a missed opportunity. Think about it. With the rise of global commerce, cross-border e-commerce platforms, and the constant buzz of social media, the way brands connect with audiences has undergone a massive transformation. Consumers aren't bound by borders anymore. With just a simple click, they can discover, explore, and even fall in love with products or services from brands thousands of miles away. And that's exactly why global marketing strategies have become not just useful—but absolutely vital—for any company that wants to stay relevant and thrive in today's dynamic economy.

Now, let's talk about the heart of a successful global brand strategy. It's a delicate dance between staying consistent and being adaptable. Your brand's core—its values, mission, and personality—should stay firm like a lighthouse guiding your journey. But how does that brand express itself? How does it speak, behave, and connect with different audiences? That needs to shift with care, with respect, and above all, with intention. Because what resonates deeply in one culture might completely miss the mark—or worse, offend—in another.

I saw this truth unfold time and again, both in my academic journey in Global Marketing at the University of Gloucestershire and during real-world experiences in India and the UK. It became clear that the brands that genuinely thrive across borders are the ones that honour local voices while staying rooted in their global identity. During our coursework and collaborations, we delved into some iconic global campaigns—Coca-Cola, Airbnb, Nike—you name it. These giants have one thing in common: they stay true to who they are while adapting how they show up in different regions. I'll never forget Coca-Cola's "Share a Coke" campaign, where they swapped out logos for names, tailoring them by country. It wasn't just clever—it was personal. And people felt it.

Here's another revelation: global marketing isn't just for the big players anymore. Thanks to tools like social media ads, influencer partnerships, and multilingual websites, even small startups and ambitious entrepreneurs can dream—and act— on a global scale. You don't need a billion-dollar war chest. What you need is clarity of vision, emotional intelligence, and a keen sense of what your audience feels, fears, and values—wherever they are.

So, if there's one truth I've learned, it's this: global marketing isn't just about spreading your message far and wide. It's about building honest, human connections with people from different walks of life. It's about nurturing relationships that last. And at the heart of it all, it's about staying rooted in your truth while reaching out with empathy and purpose.

Expanding Brand Presence Across Borders

Once you realise global marketing is a must, the next big question is: *How do you do it right?*

Spoiler alert—it's not a copy-and-paste job. Each market is its own living, breathing organism—with unique laws, expectations, preferences, humour, languages, platforms, and competition. A brand can't just show up. It has to *be understood*. And that starts with research, listening, and, above all, empathy.

In my work with brands preparing to enter international markets, we always began the same way: by running a market audit. That meant diving deep into local competition, buyer behaviour, pricing trends, platform use, and even how people consume media. Because trust me—what works like magic in the UK might get crickets in Japan. And a hero campaign in India might fall flat in Germany. Getting the local context right? It's everything.

I remember working with a health supplement brand in India that wanted to launch in the UK. On the surface, the product was great, the messaging was strong, and they were confident. But we quickly learned that the UK audience approached wellness very differently. People there were more cautious about health claims, cared a lot about sustainability and leaned into science-backed choices. So, we completely reframed the narrative—focusing on clinical research, carbon-neutral packaging, and collaborating with respected UK wellness influencers. The product itself stayed the same. But the story we told? That changed completely—and it resonated.

Today, digital tools make market expansion more agile than ever. With platforms like Shopify, Amazon Global, and social marketplaces, brands can dip their toes into international waters without drowning in costs. A smart Instagram ad, a well-localised landing page—can tell you a lot about product-market fit before you spend a pound on warehouses or supply chains.

One thing I really grew to appreciate while working in the UK's vibrant creative economy is the power of partnerships. Local agencies, micro-influencers, and even universities—they're not just allies. They're your cultural guides. They help decode the unspoken. They bring you closer to the people you're trying to reach in a way no algorithm ever could.

And here's something I can't stress enough—**compliance matters**. Every market has its own legal frameworks, and ignoring those can set your brand back months— or worse. Things like GDPR, advertising standards, and product certifications aren't checkboxes. They're trust signals. And in this era of transparency, trust is everything.

So, no, expanding across borders isn't just about being "present" in another country. It's about being *relevant*. The brands that make a real impact are the ones that take time to understand, integrate, and innovate for each market while staying rooted in who they are.

Overcoming Language and Cultural Barriers

Let's talk about the elephant in the global marketing room—language and culture.

This, more than anything, is where many brands trip up. You see, language isn't just words. It's identity. Emotion. Memory. If a brand assumes, English is enough to connect with everyone, everywhere... well, it's likely setting itself up for a harsh reality check.

I remember studying a global brand during my MBA that launched a campaign with a tagline that, when translated into Mandarin, made no sense—worse, it became a meme. It was meant to inspire but ended up confusing—and embarrassing—the brand. That experience hammered in a big lesson: machine translation is not localisation. You need real people—linguists, native speakers, cultural consultants—shaping your message at every level.

Even within the English-speaking world, tone and humour vary widely. What's clever in London might feel awkward or even offensive in New York. And something heartfelt in India could come across as overly sentimental in Australia. I've lived and worked across both Indian and UK markets, and trust me, learning to appreciate those tonal shifts is essential.

Visual culture is another piece of the puzzle. A colour like red might scream good luck in China but raise red flags elsewhere. The kind of images you use—the expressions on people's faces, how much white space you include, and even how products are styled—can all impact how your message lands. Getting these wrong doesn't just look bad; it can alienate your audience entirely.

But cultural barriers go deeper than language or imagery. They're about *values*. Rituals. Unspoken social norms. Selling luxury goods in a market that prizes modesty and minimalism? That takes tact. On the flip side, in cultures where status is celebrated, the same product might need to be positioned as aspirational and elite.

That's why I often turn to tools like the Hofstede Cultural Dimensions Model. It helps me map out how different cultures perceive things like hierarchy, risk, community, and individual expression. With this understanding, marketing messages can be crafted to connect at a much deeper, more emotional level.

For example, in Japan—a high-context culture—messages tend to be subtle, respectful, and indirect. Meanwhile, in Germany, people prefer clarity, precision, and direct communication. You can't use a one-size-fits-all script.

Above all, inclusivity and authentic representation must sit at the heart of every global marketing strategy. It's not about ticking a diversity box—it's about genuinely including and elevating diverse voices throughout your storytelling, product development, and leadership.

In the UK, especially where the creative industries thrive on multiculturalism, inclusivity is non-negotiable. It's not just ethical. It's *effective*.

In today's world, brands simply can't afford to operate in silos anymore. Global marketing strategies aren't just about growth—they're about long-term survival and relevance.

As we've explored in this section, succeeding in global markets takes more than shipping a product overseas. It demands humility, curiosity, and a willingness to learn. It's about adapting, listening, and sometimes unlearning what you thought you knew.

Language, in this journey, isn't just a tool—it's a bridge. And culture? It's not a barrier—it's an invitation. An invitation to connect more meaningfully, more respectfully, and more creatively than ever before.

From the tech corridors of India to the creative boardrooms of the UK, I've come to see that global branding isn't about being everywhere. It's about *belonging* wherever you are.

The creative corridor isn't just a pathway—it's a mindset. A commitment to empathy, connection, and evolution. And are the brands willing to embrace this? They won't just expand across borders. They'll shape the future.

Localization for Global Markets

We live in a world where borders are starting to feel more like distant memories. The rapid pace of communication, the ease of global commerce, and the incredible blend of cultures happening all around us are making it harder to draw those lines that once separated markets. It's exciting, but it also means that the old idea of "global branding" is no longer enough to make a real impact.

Let's be honest for a second: the concept of a one-size-fits-all branding approach? It's outdated, and more than that, it's risky. Brands that try to apply the same message, the same image, and the same tone across every country and culture are walking a fine line. If you really want your brand to connect with people on a global scale, it's not just about reaching more markets. It's about learning how to walk that tightrope—how to stay true to who you are as a brand while also being able to speak directly to the heart of each local culture you're entering.

This isn't something that can be figured out overnight. This balancing act—this beautiful, complex dance of localization—is what separates good international brands from truly great ones. Great brands understand that globalization doesn't mean one voice; it means many voices harmonized together.

I've been lucky enough to live and work in two vastly different yet equally dynamic markets—India and the UK. These two places are worlds apart, but the one thing they have in common is the incredible richness of their cultures. And over the years, I've come to believe with absolute certainty that localization isn't some marketing trick, some buzzword that's thrown around to make things sound fancy. It's a mindset. It's a way of thinking about your brand in a way that allows you to remain relevant, meaningful, and deeply connected to people from all walks of life. It's a strategic pillar for any brand that wants to stay true to itself while resonating with diverse audiences across the globe.

But here's the thing: localization is not just about translating a few words into a different language or swapping out imagery for something that's culturally appropriate. No. It's about reimagining everything about your brand through a local lens.

From the words you use to the visuals you choose, everything has to be carefully considered. It's about more than just adapting a message—it's about creating an experience that speaks to the local identity and values of the people you're trying to reach. The way you position your brand, the values you promote, even the emotions you evoke—all of it has to align with the cultural context you're operating in.

And when you do this, right? It's transformative. It's not just a tweak here and there, not just a nod to local customs. It's about embedding the essence of that culture into the very fabric of your brand.

Think about it for a second: you wouldn't expect a local diner in your hometown to serve the same food, in the same style, with the same presentation as a restaurant in another country, right? Even though they're both serving food, their approaches have to be different. The local diner might serve comfort food that's nostalgic to the people there, while the restaurant in another country might offer more experimental dishes based on local ingredients. Both are authentic to their environments, both are unique, and both speak to the local culture and tastes. The same should be true for brands.

Localization starts with deep listening and understanding. It's not about coming in with a pre-packaged solution and slapping it on whatever market you're targeting. You've got to dig deeper. You've got to listen to the people, understand their values, their humour, their lifestyle. What resonates with them? What challenges do they face? What makes them laugh, cry, or feel empowered? This is the heart of localization.

I've seen it firsthand in both India and the UK. In India, humour plays a huge role in everyday life—whether it's in advertisements, social media, or conversation. Indian culture tends to embrace boldness, playfulness, and a sense of warmth. So, when brands like McDonald's or Coca-Cola localized their marketing for India, they didn't just translate their slogans. They adapted their humour, their tone, and even the types of flavours in their products to better resonate with the local audience.

McDonald's brought in the Aloo Tikki burger, and Coca-Cola's campaigns started to reflect the joy and vibrancy of Indian festivals. It wasn't just about selling products; it was about creating an experience that felt truly Indian, one that made people feel like the brand understood them.

On the other hand, the UK is a more reserved, pragmatic market—yet it also thrives on irony, subtlety, and understatement. British humour is dry and often self-deprecating, and that's something brands have to recognize if they want to connect. Think about how brands like John Lewis or Tesco approach their campaigns. They don't bombard people with in-your-face advertising; instead, they focus on evoking emotions in a more understated, sincere way. John Lewis, in particular, has mastered the art of creating advertisements that are heartfelt yet restrained. They tap into the emotional lives of their audience without feeling like they're trying too hard. In this market, subtlety and empathy go a long way.

Now, I'm not saying that localization should completely change your brand's identity. In fact, it's quite the opposite. Localization isn't about changing who you are; it's about making sure that who you are comes through clearly in every market you enter. It's about finding the balance between your brand's global identity and the unique local culture you're trying to serve.

Here's where it gets tricky, though. Sometimes, the balance can feel almost impossible to strike. You might be tempted to overdo the localization to the point where it feels like you're no longer representing your brand's core. Or maybe you're so attached to your global identity that you resist change altogether. The key is finding that sweet spot where your brand stays true to its values but also shows a genuine understanding of the culture it's engaging with.

When you get it right, the rewards are huge. Localization builds trust. It makes people feel seen and understood. It shows that you've invested time and thought into the market and that you're not just there to sell but to connect. And the best part? When a brand can do this across multiple markets, it becomes a true global leader—one that people admire, one that has staying power, and one that leaves a lasting impact.

So, what does it really take to succeed with localization?

It takes empathy. It takes a willingness to learn and adapt. It takes understanding that people from different cultures have different needs, different desires, and different ways of seeing the world. And it takes the courage to be authentic, even if that means stepping outside your comfort zone.

Localization isn't just a strategy for market entry—it's a long-term commitment. When done right, it allows a brand to become a true part of people's lives, not just a product they buy. It allows a brand to evolve and grow with its audience instead of trying to force a square peg into a round hole.

Because when your brand can authentically connect with people on a local level— while still staying true to its global essence—that's when the magic happens. That's when you go beyond just selling products and begin creating relationships, creating trust, and building a community. And that's how you make your brand something that's not just known but truly loved.

How to Stay Relevant While Going Global

Let me ask you something—how does a brand expand across borders without losing the very soul that made people love it in the first place? That's the real challenge. Going global isn't about becoming something else—it's about stretching yourself, growing, and evolving— while staying recognisable and trustworthy to the people who believed in you from the start.

What I've learned is that the key lies in developing what I call *glocal* strategies. You take the global vision and you blend it with local intelligence.

From my experience, there are three core ways to make this happen:

Cultural Immersion – You can't just glance at a culture from the outside and expect to understand it. Brands need to listen—to truly listen. They need to spend time with communities, learn their histories, observe their rituals, and respect their emotions. Research is useful, yes—but empathy? That's where the magic lies.

Local Storytelling – This one's close to my heart. People love stories. But more than that, they love stories that feel like they were written *for them*. A brand might talk about innovation and eco-consciousness in the UK, but in Southeast Asia, it might speak to family, tradition, and belonging. The heart of the story stays the same—but the language? The setting? The values? They shift beautifully to match the audience.

Flexible Branding Assets – Let your local teams breathe. Give them room to work with colours, taglines, and even product names that speak directly to their audience. You'll still be you—but now, you'll be speaking their language, too.

Here's a truth I've seen play out over and over again: people don't just buy products. They buy relevance. Especially in places like the UK, where the creative industries thrive on innovation, diversity, and value-driven narratives—brands that show cultural awareness win hearts. And once you win someone's heart? Loyalty follows.

Understanding Local Market Preferences

If you want to localize successfully, you have to go deeper than surface-level observations. Every market has its own story, shaped by history, faith, language, economics, and tradition. You can't assume. You have to explore.

And it's not just about what people buy—it's about *why* they buy and *how* they buy.

Take the UK, for example. British consumers tend to appreciate subtlety, wit, and sustainability. Authenticity matters here. Now compare that with India, where choices are often influenced by family, social proof, and smart value. It's not that one is better or worse—it's just different. And understanding that difference is everything.

Here are a few things I always keep in mind when navigating local preferences:

- **Language Nuances** – Don't be fooled into thinking English is just… English. UK English is softer and more nuanced. American English is often bolder and more confident. You need to adjust your tone, your idioms, and even your humour. It makes a difference. It builds trust.

- **Visual Aesthetics** – Colours aren't universal. Symbols don't always translate. A white-themed ad that feels pure and clean in London might symbolise mourning in parts of East Asia. Design choices carry emotional weight—don't underestimate them.

- **Holidays and Festivals** – This is a powerful one. When brands honour local celebrations, they show they care. In the UK, thoughtful campaigns around Diwali, Eid, or Bonfire Night can make people feel seen, valued, and included.

- **Economic Preferences** – Let's face it—affordability means different things to different people. In developing economies, function and price might win the day. In mature markets, people often care more about ethics, minimalism, or the prestige of the brand.

One example that always stands out for me is Netflix. The way they adapt to each market is brilliant. In the UK, you'll see their platform filled with British drama, local accents, and culturally relevant storylines. In India, it's Bollywood collaborations, regional languages, and household names. And it's not just about subtitles—it's about belonging. They're telling people, "We see you. We get you."

Case Studies of Global Brands

Sometimes, the best way to understand the real power of localization is through stories—real-world examples that show us how some of the world's most iconic brands have managed to be everywhere *without losing themselves* in the process.

Here are three brands that, in my view, have absolutely mastered the art of feeling local while being undeniably global.

1. McDonald's

Ah, McDonald's—the golden arches we all know. But have you ever noticed how different a McDonald's experience feels depending on where you are in the world?

In India, where cultural and religious values shape eating habits, you won't find a Big Mac made with beef. Instead, you'll see deliciously familiar names like the McAloo Tikki and spicy Paneer Wraps—created especially with the local palate in mind. It's not just thoughtful; it's strategic.

In the UK, McDonald's has adapted again—offering plant-based burgers and healthier options to meet growing consumer interest in sustainability and wellness. It's as if the brand is saying, *"We hear you. We understand you."*

And let's not forget the storytelling. In the UK, McDonald's ad campaigns often evoke nostalgia—those little moments of everyday British life, like shared fries on a rainy afternoon or a comforting drive-thru breakfast on a rushed morning. Meanwhile, in the Middle East, their marketing speaks with deep respect to religious traditions and family values.

That's not luck. That's localization done with heart and insight—and it's a big part of why McDonald's continues to win hearts globally.

2. Airbnb

Let's talk about **Airbnb**—because, if you've ever used it, you know that it feels... personal. It's more than just booking a place to stay. There's something about the experience that feels tailored to you as if it were created with your journey in mind. And trust me, that feeling isn't an accident. It's by design, and it's what makes Airbnb stand out in the crowded world of travel and accommodation.

What sets Airbnb apart isn't just that it's a platform for booking a room or a house—it's that it *transforms* the entire experience of travel. It understands that travel isn't just about reaching a destination; it's about how you feel along the way and how you connect with the people, the culture, and the space you're staying in.

Take Japan, for example. When you browse listings in Japan, you don't just see homes—you see a reflection of the country's cultural identity. The spaces are clean, minimalistic, and infused with a sense of traditional hospitality. You can almost feel the calm serenity that defines Japanese life in every listing. Every detail is carefully curated to make you feel like you're not just staying in a house but stepping into a world that values quiet elegance and thoughtful design.

Now, let's shift gears to France. The moment you look at Airbnb listings in France, you're swept away by romance and culture. The homes feel like they've been lifted from the pages of a storybook—charming, full of character, and radiating the kind of allure you expect from the French countryside or Parisian streets. Airbnb doesn't just show you a place to sleep; it invites you into a world of beauty, culture, and timelessness, making you feel like you're part of something bigger, something uniquely French.

Then there's the unforgettable **'Live There' campaign**—a campaign that wasn't just about selling a product but about inviting people to experience life in a new way. It wasn't about polished, staged photos of perfect places. Instead, Airbnb asked real users from all around the world to share their stories and photos. It was all about showing the real, authentic experiences that make travel *human*. The photos weren't professional or posed; they were the raw, genuine moments of people living in their temporary homes. It was about connecting with the everyday beauty of life—the way people cook in their kitchens, gather around the dinner table, or take in the view from their window.

What I love about Airbnb, and what really makes it stand out, is how they **celebrate** the places they serve. They don't just enter a market and adjust their language or add a few translations—they immerse themselves in the culture, and they make that culture the star of the show. It's not about offering a generic experience for all customers. It's about curating an experience that feels deeply *local*, deeply *human*, and deeply *personal*.

For me, Airbnb isn't just a brand that provides a service. It's a brand that truly gets it. It knows that travel isn't just about the places you visit; it's about how those places make you feel and how the people who live there can make your experience richer, more authentic, and more meaningful. Airbnb doesn't just serve a market— they **celebrate** it. And that's what makes the brand so special. It's not about offering a one-size-fits-all solution. It's about creating an experience that connects you to the essence of a place, making you feel like you've truly *lived* there, even if it's just for a few days.

3. Spotify

Let's talk about something that hits home for most of us—**music**. Because if there's one thing that speaks to the heart, it's the music we love. We all have that special playlist, that song that makes us feel like the world is right, or that one track that instantly transports us to memory. Music is deeply personal—it's the soundtrack of our lives, connecting us to who we are, where we've been, and where we're going.

Take Spotify, for example. When they decided to expand into new territories, they didn't just bring their app—they brought something more. They brought a listening experience that didn't just fit into new markets but reflected the culture, tastes, and identity of the people there. It's almost like they became part of the community, weaving themselves into the fabric of local life.

In India, for instance, Spotify didn't just offer generic playlists. Instead, they curated a treasure trove of music in local languages— Tamil, Punjabi, Malayalam—and made space for Bollywood favourites alongside newer, indie music from local artists. This was Spotify meeting the culture where it lived, not just through the music but through how they understood what people wanted to hear. It wasn't about offering global hits in a local setting—it was about offering *local* music in a way that felt authentic and fresh.

And then, let's talk about the UK. Spotify's presence there didn't just echo the global mainstream trends, but it tapped into the soul of the UK music scene. Grime artists, indie rock bands, festival-ready anthems—

they're all prominently featured, not just because they're popular, but because they *define* the cultural landscape. It's clear that Spotify doesn't just play whatever is popular. They understand what resonates with their audience—whether that's blasting beats from a UK grime artist or finding a song that will be the anthem of a summer festival.

But here's where Spotify truly excels—it's not just the music they play; it's how they position themselves. It's about more than just an algorithm deciding what's next on your playlist. Spotify partners with local influencers works to promote homegrown talent, and stays in tune with the ever-shifting cultural pulse of every region they enter. They keep their finger on the beat of what's *happening*, what people are feeling, and what's making them laugh, cry, and dance.

That's the magic of Spotify. It doesn't feel like a foreign app coming into your space. It feels like *your* app. It feels like it understands you, your mood, your preferences, and your country. It feels like a friend—always there, always on cue, and always in the know. You can scroll through their playlist recommendations and instantly recognize the mix of global and local influences that speak directly to you.

Spotify isn't just playing the hits. **It's playing your hits.** And that's what makes all the difference. It's not about being just another music streaming service—it's about building a relationship with its users and making them feel like every song, every playlist, and every recommendation is tailor-made for their tastes. That's what elevates Spotify from just an app to something that feels personal and familiar. And isn't that exactly what we all want from the music we listen to? Something that feels like it was made for us, just for this moment.

Localization as a Strategic Necessity

Let me share something I've learned, both from academic studies and hands-on experience across India and the UK: localization isn't just a checkbox in a global strategy. It's the heartbeat of relevance. When you connect with people on a cultural level—when you speak *their* language, honour *their* values, and reflect *their* world—you don't just win customers. You build trust. You earn loyalty.

That kind of emotional connection can't be faked. And in competitive, creative markets like the UK—especially in hubs like London, Bristol, and Manchester— it's essential. These places are alive with cultural diversity, artistic expression, and fast-moving consumer trends. Brands that localize with authenticity are embraced quickly. The ones that don't? They're forgotten just as fast.

To me, localization is more than a marketing tactic—it's an ethical promise. A brand that localizes is saying, *"We're not just here to sell. We're here to understand. To contribute. To belong."*

And as our global marketplace becomes more interconnected, this mindset isn't just nice to have—it's what will separate the brands that survive from the ones that lead.

Because, in the end, people don't fall in love with global brands just because they're everywhere. They fall in love with brands that feel like home—no matter where in the world they are.

The Role of Technology in Global Marketing

Technology has become the beating heart of global marketing. In today's interconnected world, where brands are no longer confined by geography, it's technology that allows marketers to reach people across continents—with speed, precision, and, perhaps most importantly, creativity.

If you're trying to build something that speaks to people in Tokyo, Toronto, and Tottenham all at once, you're going to need more than just ambition—you'll need tools, systems, and insight. From my own journey—beginning with a background in computer science and growing into a global marketing career through experiences in both India and the UK—I've seen how technology is reshaping not only what we can do as marketers but how we connect on a human level.

Whether it's AI tailoring an email just for you or analytics shaping a brand's next big move, technology is what makes modern marketing intelligent, scalable, and surprisingly personal. Let's explore the key tools driving this transformation, how personalization is becoming more culturally sensitive, and why consistency— despite all this complexity— still matters.

Tools and Platforms That Enable Global Reach

What's amazing today is that global marketing is no longer limited to big corporations with massive budgets. Technology has flattened the playing field. Now, whether you're a small startup or a multinational brand, you can tell your story to the world—if you know how to use the right tools.

a.   Digital Advertising Platforms

Platforms like Google Ads, Facebook Business Manager, LinkedIn Ads, and TikTok for Business offer targeting that once felt like science fiction. You can reach someone in Manchester who loves gardening and craft beer—or a young professional in Mumbai who shops online at midnight—simply by setting the right parameters.

The data is deep. These platforms give you real-time analytics that allows you to adjust, pivot, and refine your strategy. A UK-based fashion brand, for example, might find Instagram Reels more effective for reaching Gen Z, while in India, YouTube Shorts might spark more engagement. It's not about guessing—it's about listening through data.

b.   Global Content Management Systems (CMS)

Behind every global campaign is a powerful content system. Headless CMS platforms like Contentful, Strapi, or Adobe Experience Manager help brands separate content from design so that local teams can adapt messaging without breaking the global look and feel.

Imagine launching a global campaign where every region sees the same visual design—but the language, tone, and cultural nuances are spot on. These tools even let you automate translations and coordinate content drops across time zones, ensuring everyone feels the launch was *for them.*

c.   E-commerce and CRM Platforms

Think of Shopify Plus, Salesforce, or HubSpot—not just as sales platforms but as bridges to global audiences. They allow your e-commerce storefront to speak multiple languages, accept local currencies, and offer preferred payment methods, creating an experience that feels tailored and trustworthy.

CRM tools, meanwhile, are like your brand's memory—they remember what your customers like, how they behave, and what keeps them coming back. This helps you build relationships that aren't just transactional but emotional—and that's where brand loyalty lives.

d.   Collaboration and Workflow Tools

If you've ever worked across time zones, you know the chaos of missed messages and disjointed feedback. Tools like Slack, Notion, Trello, and Asana bring global teams together. Figma and Canva Pro for Teams let designers from different countries build visuals side by side, while translation tools like Smartling or Lokalise help ensure nothing gets lost in translation.

In short, technology hasn't just connected our audiences—it's connected *us*. It's how global brands run like local teams, no matter how far apart we are.

Personalization Across Borders

One of the most beautiful shifts in marketing today is that it's no longer about broadcasting one message to everyone. It's about speaking directly to *you*—where you are, who you are, and what matters to you.

But let's be honest: personalizing on a global scale is hard. People don't just speak different languages; they think differently, feel differently, shop differently. That's where smart technology steps in— helping us learn, adapt, and connect with nuance and care.

a.   Data Collection and Analysis

It all starts with listening. Tools like Google Analytics 4, Mixpanel, and Segment gather insights from websites, emails, social media, and even purchase patterns. And when you read that data right, the story becomes clear.

A fashion brand might notice that customers in northern England buy coats weeks before their southern counterparts. With that knowledge, they can launch early-bird campaigns, customize homepage banners, and offer tailored discounts—making customers feel understood, not targeted.

b. *AI and Machine Learning*

This is where it gets exciting. AI isn't just crunching numbers—it's learning *feelings*, patterns, and timing. Like a good friend, it remembers what you like and knows when to reach out.

Recommendation engines, like those used by Amazon or Netflix, suggest products or shows based on not just your habits—but on cultural trends and social sentiment. AI can personalize email campaigns by region, test subject lines, predict open rates, and even choose the best time to hit "send" in every country. It's not robotic. It's intuitive.

c. *Dynamic Content and Localization*

Your website can now change its face depending on who's visiting. That's dynamic content. From localised greetings to product recommendations to festival-specific promotions—it's all designed to feel personal.

Take Spotify Wrapped, for example. It's global—but deeply personal. In India, it might showcase Bollywood beats and festive flair. In the UK, it could highlight indie rock and Glastonbury nostalgia. Same platform. Different emotions. That's the magic of localization.

d. *Challenges of Global Personalization*

Of course, with power comes responsibility. Get the tone or imagery wrong, and you risk cultural missteps that can alienate rather than attract. And then there's data privacy. From GDPR in Europe to PDPA in Asia, the rules are strict—and rightly so.

Personalization must be built on trust. You can't just *know* your customer—you have to respect their privacy, their values, and their right to transparency.

When done well, personalization doesn't feel creepy. It feels caring. And that's what customers remember.

Ensuring Consistency in Global Brand Messaging

As much as technology allows us to localize and personalize, it also presents a challenge—how do you stay true to who you are as a brand while adapting to so many different audiences?

The answer lies in creating consistency—not sameness, but coherence. A brand should feel like itself, whether you're seeing it in Seoul or Sheffield.

a.   Establishing a Brand Governance Framework

This is your brand's compass. A governance model—complete with style guides, tone-of-voice documents, and visual identity rules—helps teams around the world tell the same story, even if they're speaking different dialects.

Platforms like Frontify, Bynder, or Canva Brand Kit help enforce these standards without stifling creativity. A logo may remain unchanged, but the tone might shift—a more formal style for Tokyo, a cheekier tone for London. Same voice, different inflections.

b.   Centralized Strategy, Local Execution

Think global, act local. It's not just a cliché—it's how the best brands work. The overarching strategy might come from the headquarters, but local teams should have the freedom to tailor execution.

Coca-Cola's "Share a Coke" campaign nailed this. Globally unified, yet locally beloved. The idea was the same—names on bottles—but each country featured names that resonated with their people in their language. That's consistency with a human touch.

c. Unified Technology Infrastructure

Consistency also relies on a shared foundation. A unified tech stack—same CMS, same CRM, same analytics—ensures that data, design, and decisions align across the board. This matters most in moments of urgency. When trends shift fast, or crises emerge, a connected infrastructure allows brands to respond quickly, cohesively, and confidently across all markets.

d. Monitoring and Quality Control

Staying consistent also means keeping a close eye on what's being said about your brand. Tools like Brandwatch, Mention, and Sprinklr monitor social chatter and alert you to inconsistencies, misunderstandings, or emerging issues.

With this real-time insight, you can step in, course-correct, or simply reassure your audience that, *yes, we hear you.*

Technology as the Backbone of Global Marketing

Let's dive into something that's close to my heart—**technology**. Now, when you think about global marketing, you might imagine grand campaigns, massive outreach efforts, and far-reaching ads. And while all of that is true, there's another side to the story. You see, technology hasn't just made global marketing possible— it's made it **personal, predictive**, and **powerful**. It's no longer just about reaching the masses; it's about truly connecting with individuals, even when those individuals are on the other side of the globe.

Think about it: we now have digital platforms that enable brands to connect with audiences no matter where they are. Whether it's through social media, personalized emails, or tailored ad campaigns, technology has broken down the barriers of geography. What was once a world where brands could only speak to specific regions or cultures has transformed into one where your brand can touch lives all over the world. Yet, it's not just about reaching a wider audience. It's about **making sure you're connecting with them** on a deeper, more intimate level.

Let me explain it from my own perspective. From my early days coding algorithms, where numbers and logic were my closest companions, to now telling stories that resonate with people—one thing has always stood out: **technology and creativity are not opposites**. They don't cancel each other out. In fact, they *complement* each other in ways that can change the way brands interact with the world. I've seen it firsthand in the UK's creative economy, where this union of technology and creativity doesn't just set trends—it sets the pace for **true innovation**.

Technology helps brands **predict** what audiences need, understand their preferences, and even anticipate their desires before they fully realize them. It's what turns a simple customer interaction into a meaningful exchange. It makes sure that your marketing doesn't just reach someone—it speaks to them personally, showing them that you understand them, their needs, and their world. It takes the mass appeal of global marketing and transforms it into something that feels tailored and special, something that feels as though the brand is truly listening to you.

And let me tell you, in this interconnected world, it's technology that ensures your voice is heard—**clearly, consistently, and with care**. In the past, brands could afford to simply shout into the void. But today, with every tweet, every post, every click, there's an opportunity for brands to listen, to engage, and to show that they're paying attention. Global brands no longer just speak loudly—they speak wisely. They take the time to understand the nuances of different cultures, languages, and even the emotional needs of their audiences. And they listen. They listen to what their customers are saying, whether it's through direct feedback, social media interactions, or behavioural data.

In this landscape, technology isn't just an add-on. It's the backbone that holds everything together. Without it, the journey to building global connections would be like sailing without a compass—unknowing, uncertain, and unpredictable. But with it, brands can chart a course, stay on track, and navigate the vast seas of global markets, all while making sure their message is heard and felt by each individual in a personal, meaningful way. It's this blend of technology and creativity that's changing the face of global marketing, making it not just possible but profoundly impactful.

Chapter 4

London and the UK – Creative Capitals

The UK's Creative Edge

There's something about the **United Kingdom**, particularly **London** that strikes a chord deep within you. It's a feeling that goes beyond words, a sensation that's hard to define but one that you *know* in your bones. If you've ever wandered through London's cobbled streets or taken a quiet moment in one of its bustling squares, you understand exactly what I mean. It's a city where creativity is not just an idea—it's an energy that pulses through every corner, in every conversation, and within every creative act.

You can feel this energy in the way **The Beatles'** music echoes through side streets as if the sound of their songs has become a permanent part of the city's soundtrack. Their music doesn't just remind you of a bygone era—it connects you to a time when creativity had the power to change the world. There's something magical about how their tunes still manage to stir the heart of a city, making you realise that even decades later, their creativity lives on.

And then, there's the street art—the powerful **Banksy murals** scattered across the city. Each one feels like a statement, a quiet rebellion against the status quo. These pieces of art aren't just for admiring; they're meant to provoke thought to challenge what we take for granted. They invite you to see the world through a different lens, pushing the boundaries of creativity and forcing you to question the world around you. **Banksy's** work isn't just about art; it's about culture, social change, and using creativity as a weapon for expression.

On the flip side, creativity in the UK is also embodied in its elegance—take, for instance, the **Burberry** brand. With each runway show, each new collection, it's not just fashion that's being paraded. It's a **legacy** of British creativity, where craftsmanship, design, and heritage come together to form something timeless. You can't help but feel pride when you see a Burberry piece because it's not just about the clothes— it's about the history and the culture behind them. This is a country that knows how to marry tradition with innovation, where the past inspires the future.

Then there's **British Vogue**, a symbol of the UK's creative prowess, where **fashion** isn't merely a business—it's an art form. The glossy pages of the magazine aren't just filled with trends—they're filled with a vision of the future. British Vogue has the remarkable ability to take something as ephemeral as fashion and turn it into a statement about culture, identity, and society. It's a place where the boundaries between art, fashion, and personal expression blur, and in doing so, it influences millions of people worldwide.

But here's the thing: this isn't just a country that **supports** creativity. The UK *does* creativity. It's part of the air you breathe when you walk through the streets of London or any city in the UK. Creativity is woven into the fabric of everyday life. It's not just about art galleries or fashion shows—it's about the *everyday* person who brings their creativity into their work, their relationships, and their passions. It's the way people approach problem-solving. It's how new ideas are welcomed, tested, and pushed to their limits. It's a culture that says, "Be bold. Be original. Take risks." And then it provides the resources and support to help you turn your dreams into reality.

The creativity here isn't confined to one space or one sector. It's a **force** that moves through **glass-fronted studios** where fresh ideas are born into the **late-night cafés** where artists, writers, and musicians come together to share their dreams over cups of coffee. It moves from **lecture halls**, where young minds challenge the status quo, to the **city streets**, where every corner might offer the next big idea. The UK is a place where every encounter, every exchange, feels like an opportunity for **creativity to thrive**.

And, let me tell you from experience: if you've ever spent time in this creative ecosystem—whether in a brainstorming session with colleagues or in a casual chat with a stranger turned collaborator—you will know the undeniable truth: the UK doesn't just talk about creativity. It **celebrates** it. It offers it a seat at the table, and it listens. The whole country seems to be in conversation, constantly feeding and nourishing new ideas. It's not just about being creative—it's about **living** creatively in everything you do.

And that's where it gets interesting. Because when you step into the world of **global marketing**, the UK doesn't just serve as a location on a map. It serves as a **compass**. It points you in the right direction, helping you navigate the complexities of creativity, culture, and commerce. It inspires you to push the boundaries of what you thought was possible and to reach for the kind of creativity that can truly transform the world.

As someone who's sat in many of these creative spaces, argued passionately for an idea, or shared a quiet moment of inspiration with someone who was once a stranger, I can tell you with absolute certainty—this country doesn't just produce creativity. It **cultivates** it. And if you're on a journey of discovery, of **global marketing**, the UK is the perfect place to help you find your way.

Let me show you why.

To truly understand the unique position the UK holds in the world's creative landscape, you have to appreciate the **interplay of history, culture, and cutting-edge thinking** that permeates every aspect of British life. From Shakespeare's plays to the revolutionary works of the **Beatles**, creativity has always been a thread that binds this island together. It's a thread that has been passed down through generations, evolving and expanding, yet never losing its power to captivate, inspire, and transform.

In **London**, the capital city, you can feel the creative pulse vibrate through every corner. The **cityscape** itself—a blend of historic monuments and contemporary architectural marvels—is a living testament to how creativity continuously adapts and pushes boundaries. Whether you're standing on the **Southbank**, gazing out at the majestic River Thames, or walking through the vibrant **Shoreditch** streets filled with street art and design studios, you'll find a city that thrives on innovation.

The UK's creativity isn't confined to a single genre, industry, or medium—it transcends them. The **music, art, fashion, film**, and **technology** sectors are interconnected in a way that only a culture rich in diversity and history can truly achieve. The creative sectors in the UK have the unique ability to absorb and merge various influences—from **classical British traditions** to the **globalization** of the digital age— and turn them into something new, exciting, and relevant.

Take, for example, the music industry: London has been home to iconic acts like **The Beatles**, **The Rolling Stones**, and **Amy Winehouse**, but it is also where a new generation of musicians is redefining what it means to be an artist in the 21st century. From **grime** and **indie** to **electronic music** and **pop**, the UK is a hotbed of musical talent that resonates with audiences far beyond its borders. The way British musicians blend genres, challenge conventions, and constantly push the boundaries of creativity is an indicator of the kind of innovative spirit that pervades the country.

In **fashion**, the UK is home to **trendsetters** who marry boldness with sophistication, all while drawing upon the nation's rich history of textile craftsmanship. The name **Burberry** alone evokes an image of British elegance, but the UK fashion scene isn't confined to high-end brands. From the street style of **East London** to the avant-garde designs showcased during **London Fashion Week**, creativity in the UK constantly evolves, telling stories that reflect the changing societal and cultural landscape.

But it's not just the **arts** that are thriving in the UK. The creative sector in **business and marketing** is one of the **most dynamic** in the world. The way UK businesses have been able to **blend tradition with modern innovation** is a huge factor in the country's global influence. Whether it's through cutting-edge **tech startups** in **Silicon Roundabout** or world-leading advertising agencies that build brands with a profound sense of **storytelling**, the UK's business landscape is one where creative thinking is at the core of success.

Perhaps the most telling sign of the UK's creative edge is its ability to remain a beacon for **global talent**. In a world where borders are becoming less rigid and competition for talent is fierce, the UK continues to attract creatives, innovators, and visionaries from across the globe. The country offers a rich ecosystem of **opportunities, networks**, and **resources** that allow ideas to flourish and transform into something larger than life.

This section is a celebration of the **UK's creative edge**. It's about understanding the roots of this creativity, how it manifests in every corner of society, and why this country is a **magnet for innovation**. As we explore the UK's creative journey, I invite you to take a closer look at how this edge has **shaped the way we approach marketing**, **branding**, and even **technology**. The UK's creativity is not just a byproduct of its history—it is **woven into its DNA**, and it continues to **reshape the global marketing landscape** in bold and unexpected ways.

As we journey through this section, let's examine what makes the **UK's creative edge** so influential and how you can tap into this energy to fuel your own creative endeavours. From **art** to **commerce**, **music** to **tech**, the UK offers a template for integrating creativity and innovation into every facet of our professional and personal lives.

Welcome to the creative world of the UK—where the possibilities are as endless as the ideas waiting to be explored.

Marketing and Innovation in the UK Why London is a Global Marketing Hub

To truly understand why **London** stands out as a global marketing hub, you need to look beyond the obvious—the iconic red buses, the ever-photogenic skyline, and the familiar landmarks that seem to be on every postcard. Don't get me wrong, those things are beautiful, but they don't tell the full story. The real magic, the true heart of London, lies in something much more profound: **its people**.

Walk through the streets of London, and you'll notice it almost immediately. The city hums with an energy that comes from a **mash-up of cultures**, an intricate tapestry of experiences and stories, each one bringing something unique to the table. It's in the way different lives intersect, how you can be standing in the middle of one neighbourhood and hear a language you've never heard before. It's in the way a warm breeze can carry the rhythm of a thousand accents—each one a note in the city's symphony. From the bustling markets to the quiet corners of neighbourhood cafes, there's always something happening here. It's a place where you're never really alone. Even in a crowd, there's a sense of belonging.

What makes London stand apart is its **human diversity**—and I'm not just talking about the diversity of faces or backgrounds, but the diversity of thought. When you bring people from all over the world into one place, something beautiful happens. The city becomes a **melting pot of creativity**, where ideas collide and spark in unexpected ways. People from different cultures, with different ways of seeing the world, come together to create something new, something that might not have existed otherwise. This is the secret behind London's magnetic appeal. It's not just about business, marketing, or the economy. It's about how those things are **shaped** and **inspired** by the people who live and work here.

And this is where London's power as a global marketing hub comes into play. In a city so rich in diversity, **creativity flows freely**. There's a freedom to explore new concepts, experiment with fresh ideas, and push boundaries without fear of being confined to a single narrative or viewpoint. The **ideas that rise from London's streets** have the potential to travel far because they are born from a place that isn't afraid to challenge norms, embrace change, and welcome the unexpected.

It's this blend of culture, diversity, and open-mindedness that makes London such a force in the world of marketing. When you create something here, you know it's been influenced by so many different perspectives that it has the power to resonate with people everywhere—whether they're in New York, Paris, Tokyo, or Johannesburg. London's creative pulse beats with the knowledge that every corner of the globe is within reach. And that's what makes it such an exciting, inspiring place to be.

So, when you think about why London is at the heart of global marketing, don't just think of its landmarks. Think of the people, the stories, the dreams, and the voices that come together here, creating a unique mix of ideas and opportunities that can shape the future. That's London's secret: its people and the **infinite possibilities they create** together.

1. A Magnet for Global Talent

London calls to creatives across the world. I've crossed paths with designers from Delhi, filmmakers from Paris, strategists from Johannesburg, and copywriters from São Paulo. All of them are drawn to this city, walking the same corridors, bouncing ideas off each other, and pitching campaigns that are woven with global experiences. And that shared spirit—that richness—is what makes this place extraordinary.

What strikes me most is how the UK doesn't just "accept" emerging fields like immersive media or AI storytelling—it embraces them with open arms. If you're craving space to experiment, to fail spectacularly and rise again, London gives you that space. It hands you the brush and says, "Paint something no one's seen before."

2. Access to Global Clients and Markets

Here's what makes London exhilarating: it's a place where decisions that shape the world are made. Giants like Google, Facebook, Unilever, and Nike don't just have offices here—they make their European homes in this city. And for marketers and creatives, that means our ideas aren't confined to back rooms. They're launched into boardrooms that span the globe.

Add to that London's time zone sweet spot—you start your day with Tokyo and wrap it with New York. It's not just convenient. It shapes your thinking. It forces you to understand, to empathise, and to create stories that transcend borders.

3. Creative Clusters and Innovation Hubs

Every corner of London seems to sing its own creative melody. Take Soho—where advertising legends haunt every pub and the air buzzes with storytelling. Then there's Shoreditch, once gritty and forgotten, now a kaleidoscope of indie agencies, neon-lit co-working spaces, and tech startups daring to dream.

These aren't just working spaces—they're where ideas collide. I once watched a sustainability activist and a UX designer spark a campaign idea over coffee. That's London for you—a living, breathing moodboard.

4. Supportive Policy and Investment

Creativity doesn't thrive on passion alone. It needs scaffolding, and the UK provides it. With tax reliefs, innovation grants, and funding from champions like Arts Council England, Creative UK, and Innovate UK, this country understands that creative work is both cultural and commercial capital.

And then there's the stage: London Fashion Week, Clerkenwell Design Week, and Ad Week Europe. These events aren't just spectacles—they're launchpads. They give bold ideas a global spotlight. If you're a marketer wanting to be seen, this is your runway.

Major Creative Agencies and Their Impact

Now, let's talk about the powerhouses—the agencies that don't just sell products but rewrite narratives. These aren't just offices filled with creatives. They are temples of thought, of emotion, of innovation.

1. WPP

WPP isn't a company—it's a universe. With Ogilvy, Grey, VMLY&R, and Wunderman Thompson under its umbrella, it shapes not only ads but perspectives.

Their work? It's where strategy kisses the soul. Dove's "Real Beauty." Guinness's cinematic epics. These aren't just campaigns— they're cultural artefacts. WPP shows us what happens when data and empathy hold hands.

2. Saatchi & Saatchi

This name echoes through time. From the unforgettable "Labour Isn't Working" poster to Visa's global campaigns, Saatchi & Saatchi crafts narratives that stick in your chest.

I've seen their purpose-driven campaigns move people to tears—and action. Their work doesn't sell. It sings. It stirs. It stands for something.

3. BBH (Bartle Bogle Hegarty)

"When the world zigs, zag." That's not just BBH's motto—it's a way of life. Their simplicity cuts through the noise. Their humour disarms. Their honesty lingers.

From Audi's truth-telling to Levi's soul-searching, BBH makes us feel, and that's what great marketing is about—reminding us we're human.

4. Mother London

If agencies had personalities, Mother would be the rule-breaking, heart-thumping creative you can't stop thinking about. Bold. Honest. Unapologetically real.

Their work for IKEA, Uber Eats, and Stella Artois is unpredictable in the best way. They don't just create campaigns—they craft memories. The kind you quote. The kind that makes you smile unexpectedly on a rainy Tuesday.

These agencies aren't just industry leaders—they're cultural architects. They ask better questions. They challenge the status quo. And if you're lucky enough to work with them, you don't just create—you evolve.

Lessons from UK's Creative Landscape

The Role of Universities and Institutions in Creative Growth

Behind every iconic ad or stirring brand story is a person—a curious, persistent soul shaped by education, by mentors, and by long nights driven by dreams and caffeine. The UK's creative strength has deep roots, and it starts with how it teaches its thinkers to think.

1. Top Creative Institutions

- *University of the Arts London (UAL):* Home to Central Saint Martins and other legends, UAL isn't just a university—it's a launchpad. When you walk through its halls, you can almost hear Alexander McQueen whispering to the next genius in line.

- *Royal College of Art (RCA):* RCA is where ideas get serious. It's not about pretty pictures. It's about reshaping how we see the world—through research, through experimentation, through fearless invention.

- *Goldsmiths, University of London:* If you want a place where curiosity is sacred and questioning the norm is the norm, Goldsmiths is it. It nurtures misfits, visionaries, and cultural critics all at once.

- *London College of Communication (LCC):* Nestled within UAL, LCC is a pipeline to the industry. Future journalists, advertisers, and digital creators find their footing here— guided by real briefs and real stakes.

These schools aren't just institutions—they're incubators of possibility. They give students mentors, platforms, and the courage to push boundaries.

2. Industry Partnerships and Real-World Learning

One of the things I admire most is how these universities blur the line between classroom and boardroom. Students pitch to real clients, solve real problems, and build confidence not from textbooks—but from experience.

I'll never forget watching a young student pitch a campaign to an agency veteran— and seeing that shift. That flash of belief. That moment when a student realised, "I can do this."

3. Research, Innovation, and Thought Leadership

British institutions are shaping what comes next. Whether it's how brands use VR, how they embrace ethics, or how design can save the planet, the UK is leading.

Initiatives like the Creative Clusters project bring together academia, industry, and government to explore what the future of creative business might look like. It's not about trends—it's about transformation.

A Global Beacon for Creativity

London and the UK—they don't just sit back, content with what they've achieved. They don't simply bask in the glow of their rich history, relying on the weight of the past to carry them forward. No, this place does something remarkable. It takes its history—its legacy—and builds on it, continually pushing boundaries, forging ahead, and reimagining what's possible. It's the pulse of innovation, an unyielding force that constantly seeks new heights yet never forgets where it came from. And that's what makes this place truly special. It's the perfect fusion of past and future, tradition and disruption, local roots and global ambition.

I want to take you deeper into what makes this part of the world such a beacon for creativity. If you've ever visited London, or the UK in general, you'll know what I'm talking about. It's hard to define it with words—there's this energy in the air, a feeling that creativity isn't just something we do but something we *are*. Creativity is embedded in the very fabric of life here, from the tiniest street corner to the grandest institutions, from the local cafés to the boardrooms of global giants. It's alive and breathing in every conversation, every meeting, every collaboration. It doesn't just exist in the minds of artists, writers, or musicians. It's in the hearts and hands of everyone. Whether you're a teacher, a lawyer, or a marketing professional—creativity is part of the daily rhythm of life.

For those of us in marketing, coming to the UK is more than just a career move. It's an immersion. It's stepping into a world where creativity is currency, where it's valued above all else. Here, collaboration isn't something you have to work at or try to cultivate—it's instinct. It's in the air, in the way people approach problems and solutions. There's a shared understanding that we're all in this together, constantly pushing each other to be better, think bigger, and reach further. It's the kind of environment that makes you feel alive, that sparks your imagination at every turn.

And then there's the culture. Oh, the culture! The UK doesn't just create—it *breathes* creativity. It's woven into the country's very DNA. From Shakespeare's plays to the punk revolution, from fashion icons to cutting-edge digital art, the UK has always been at the forefront of cultural movements. And it hasn't slowed down. Every day, new ideas are born here, nurtured, and given the freedom to evolve. Whether it's the latest marketing trend, a new tech startup, or an avant-garde piece of art in a gallery, London and the UK continue to be the birthplace of bold, game-changing ideas.

I think it's important to mention something that can sometimes get lost in translation for those outside of the UK: here, creativity isn't just about coming up with the next big thing. It's about daring to ask questions that no one has thought to ask. It's about seeing the world in a way that no one else has dared to. It's about challenging norms, breaking down barriers, and embracing failure as a stepping stone to something bigger and better. There's no room for complacency. Creativity here doesn't settle for the ordinary—it demands the extraordinary.

In fact, if there's one thing I've learned from my own journey here, it's this: in the UK, creativity isn't just a job or a skill—it's a way of life. It's the lens through which people see the world. It's how they feel, how they think, how they connect with each other and the world around them. Creativity here isn't just about coming up with something new or innovative. It's about feeling the pulse of the world, understanding its rhythms, and contributing to the ever-evolving story of humanity.

Once you've experienced that kind of energy, once you've truly tasted the magic of a place that values creativity so deeply, you can't unsee it. It stays with you and follows you wherever you go. It doesn't matter where your journey takes you— once creativity becomes part of who you are, it never leaves. It's woven into the fabric of your thoughts, your work, and your story. And that's the beauty of it. It's something that doesn't just belong to a city, a country, or even a culture. It belongs to all of us who are brave enough to embrace it, to let it shape our worlds, our businesses, and our lives.

In London and the UK, the message is clear: creativity is not an afterthought. It's the driving force behind everything. From startups to legacy brands, from the streets to the stage, the emphasis is on making things that matter, that resonate, and that create lasting impact. And for those of us in the marketing world, it's an incredible opportunity. We're not just selling products or services—we're telling stories, crafting experiences, and building connections that will shape the future.

So, what does that mean for you? It means that if you're looking to make your mark in this world, to leave a lasting impact, the UK is the place to be. Here, you're not just another marketer; you're part of a movement. You're a creator, a disruptor, a pioneer. Whether you're working with global brands or local startups, you're at the heart of a creative revolution, one that's happening right now. The UK isn't just about a place—it's about a mindset, a culture, and an energy that encourages us all to push boundaries, explore new ideas, and be unapologetically bold in our work.

And the beauty of it? That energy, that creative spark, isn't confined to the streets of London. It's a mindset that can travel with you no matter where you go. So, whether you're here for a short while or for the long haul, know this: once you've experienced this creative spirit, you carry it with you always. It's not just something you learn. It's something you become.

Because here's the thing: creativity is contagious. And once it's in your blood, it shapes everything you do, everywhere you go. And that's something truly extraordinary.

Chapter 5

The Power of Story in Strategy: Why Storytelling Matters More Than Ever

In today's world, it often feels like we're drowning in a sea of endless content. Everywhere you look, there's something new: **offers, advertisements, headlines,** and **endless choices,** all fighting for a piece of your attention. It's overwhelming, isn't it? The noise is deafening. But here's the truth—there's one thing that rises above it all, one force that always seems to break through the chaos, and that is **storytelling**.

Now, let me pause for a second and really emphasize this point: storytelling is not just another marketing tool. It's so much more than that. In the world of branding, it's the **soul** of what makes a brand *real* and *relatable*. It's the bridge that connects businesses to their audiences on a deeper, more personal level. When you tell a good story, you're not just selling a product or service—you're creating something far greater. You're crafting an **identity**, an **experience**, a **culture** that people can relate to and want to be a part of. It's through storytelling that a brand begins to resonate with us emotionally, forming connections that go beyond mere transactions.

Let's face it—people don't just buy products; they buy into **stories**. Think about the brands you love. I'm sure there's something about their story—their history, their mission, or the way they make you feel—that makes you come back to them again and again. It's not just about the product's features or the price tag—it's the **narrative** that surrounds it. It's how the story makes you feel, how it sparks memories, or how it aligns with your personal values. And that's the power of a good story— it has the ability to create an emotional bond with your audience that can last long after the sale.

In this section, I want to walk you through why **storytelling** is such a game-changer in the marketing world. I'll share with you how powerful

69

narratives can shape perceptions and influence decisions. I'll also dive into the process of **weaving** your own stories—stories that not only capture attention but also form real, meaningful connections with your audience. Because, when you connect on an emotional level, that's when the magic happens. That's when you create not just customers but **loyal advocates** who believe in your brand, who trust you, and who will carry your story forward.

It's time to realize that storytelling isn't just about telling *any* story—it's about telling a **compelling**, **authentic** story that your audience can feel. This is what will truly set you apart in a crowded market and make your brand unforgettable. Let's dig deeper into why storytelling should be at the heart of your marketing strategy and how you can start crafting narratives that will leave a lasting impact.

Storytelling in Marketing

1. Why Storytelling is the Heart of Branding

a) Stories Humanize Brands

Think about it—people don't connect with logos. They connect with the emotions, journeys, and values behind them. Storytelling breathes life into a brand, giving it a human voice that resonates with audiences. Take Apple, for instance—not just a tech brand, but the rebellious spirit that pushes creativity. Or Nike—not merely a sportswear brand but a symbol of perseverance, struggle, and triumph. These aren't just clever marketing strategies; they are stories built over time that reflect deeper values.

Especially in multicultural environments like the UK, a strong brand story serves as a bridge. It transcends demographics and speaks directly to shared human experiences. Whether it's a global initiative or a hyper-local campaign, stories have this magical way of making brands feel personal, even intimate.

b) Stories Offer Meaning and Purpose

In a marketplace flooded with products, consumers are seeking more than just material goods—they're looking for meaning. They want brands that stand for something. Storytelling is the perfect vehicle to express this purpose. Patagonia, for example, doesn't just sell outdoor gear; its story speaks volumes about environmental advocacy, creating trust and authenticity in ways no ad ever could. This kind of alignment is priceless—it goes far beyond the superficiality of products and taps directly into the heart.

c) Stories Drive Brand Recall

Here's something that'll stick with you: research shows that we're 22 times more likely to remember a fact if it's wrapped in a story. That's huge! In the world of marketing, this means that stories don't just create memories—they create lasting connections. Whether it's through a powerful video, a heartfelt testimonial, or a customer journey, a well-told story plants a seed in the consumer's mind, anchoring the brand in their memory. It's not about a transaction anymore; it's about a story they'll remember.

2. Crafting Stories that Resonate with Audiences

a) Know Your Audience Deeply

Here's the secret sauce—empathy. To create a story that resonates, you have to understand your audience at a deep, human level. This goes far beyond basic demographics. You need to know their hopes, fears, struggles, and dreams.

Take John Lewis, for example. Their famous Christmas ads aren't about selling products—they're about telling stories that capture the essence of British culture and the emotions that surround the holidays. They've nailed the art of storytelling that feels personal, year after year because they truly understand what touches their audience.

b) Structure is Everything

A good story isn't random—it has structure. Think of it like a well-crafted recipe: you need the right ingredients and the perfect balance. Most great stories follow a simple structure:

- **The protagonist** (usually the customer, not the brand)

- **The challenge** (a problem your audience can relate to)

- **The solution** (how your brand helps solve that problem)

- **The transformation** (what success looks like after using the brand)

Airbnb's campaigns, for instance, often feature real stories from hosts and travellers. The beauty of these stories is in their authenticity—they show real struggles and meaningful outcomes, inviting audiences to feel like part of a community.

c) *Authenticity Over Perfection*

Let's face it: today's audiences are savvy. They can sniff out overly polished, "too good to be true" stories from miles away. The real magic happens when brands embrace **raw**, **real**, and **relatable** narratives. It's about being genuine, not perfect.

Look at Dove's "Real Beauty" campaign—it's grounded in authenticity. They featured real women, not models, creating a conversation around beauty standards that resonates on a global scale. Authentic stories like these spark connections because they reflect real life, not a fabricated ideal.

3. The Emotional Connection Between Brands and Consumers

a) *Emotion Drives Action*

Here's the big takeaway: **emotion drives action**. While logic informs, it's the emotion that pushes people to act. Neuromarketing studies show that emotional responses

are far more influential than the content of the ad itself. When people feel something, they're more likely to take action.

Take Google's "Parisian Love" ad—it's simple but deeply emotional, drawing people in with its sincerity and authenticity. This kind of emotional connection doesn't just make people feel something; it drives them to engage, share, and remember. And that's the kind of loyalty that builds long-lasting brands.

b) Building Community Through Shared Stories

When customers see their own values reflected in a brand's story, they don't just buy into the brand—they buy into a community. This feeling of belonging is something special. Brands like LEGO, for example, have turned storytelling into a way to bring people together. They invite fans to share their creations, creating a community of engaged brand advocates.

In today's world, where connection and collaboration are key, storytelling becomes more than just a way to communicate—it becomes a tool for building relationships.

c) Emotional Resonance in a Global Market

When storytelling crosses borders, it taps into something universal: emotion. Yet, we must acknowledge that the way emotion is expressed can vary culturally. What resonates in the UK might not land the same way in another country. This is where the magic of **localized storytelling** comes in.

Look at Coca-Cola's "Share a Coke" campaign. The core message—sharing and personalization—was universal, but the execution was adapted for each market. It felt both global and local at the same time.

In the UK, for example, campaigns that reflect British humour, nostalgia, and pride tend to resonate deeply. Think about British Airways' "A British Original" campaign—there's something about it that feels distinctly British, yet universally emotional. It's this balance that makes global storytelling so powerful.

Telling Stories That Stick

In the digital age, where content is consumed in seconds and forgotten just as quickly, storytelling is not a luxury—it's a necessity. It is the soul of a brand's strategy, the bridge between marketing and meaning. As we've seen, storytelling humanizes brands, creates emotional bonds, and transforms customers into loyal advocates.

For marketers operating in global environments—especially within the creative epicentres like London and across the UK—the ability to tell stories that resonate across cultures is a defining skill. It's no longer about the product alone; it's about the world the brand invites you into.

As we move deeper into the creative economy, the brands that will lead are those who understand this simple truth: the best marketing isn't a pitch—it's a story well told.

Content That Speaks to the Soul

In today's digital ecosystem, content is everywhere—scrolling feeds, autoplay ads, reels, stories, pop-ups, and emails. Yet, despite the ocean of messaging, only a few drops truly reach the audience in a meaningful way. Why? Because most content talks at people, not to them. It focuses on conversion before connection visibility before value. But a quiet revolution is underway—where soulful content, shaped by genuine stories and empathy, cuts through the noise.

This section explores the transformation from transactional messaging to human storytelling. We'll unpack why soul-stirring content is the new competitive edge, how to use storytelling to uncover audience needs, and why authenticity—not perfection—is the ultimate driver of engagement.

1. The Shift from Selling to Storytelling

a) *From Features to Feelings*

Traditional marketing focused on selling features—how fast a phone charged, how soft a fabric felt, or how long a battery lasted. While those elements are still relevant, they no longer define a brand. In a world where experience trumps explanation, storytelling wins hearts before minds.

Think about the way Airbnb tells its story. Rather than focus solely on properties, it sells the experience of belonging anywhere. The marketing isn't just about a bed or a room—it's about connection, discovery, and freedom. This is the power of moving from hard facts to human feelings.

b) *From Transaction to Relationship*

Modern consumers expect more than just a product—they want to feel understood. Brands are no longer simply vendors; they're relationship-builders. And just like in human relationships, stories are the foundation.

Storytelling offers continuity. It's not a single touchpoint—it's an evolving narrative that builds trust over time. A great brand doesn't just show up during a sale; it becomes part of the customer's life journey. Consider Nike—a brand that's not about shoes but about the journey of every athlete, every effort, and every obstacle overcome.

This strategic narrative approach enables brands to become emotional companions, not just commercial entities.

c) *From Audience to Co-creators*

In the creative economy, brands don't just tell stories—they invite audiences to be part of them. Whether it's user-generated content, reviews, or testimonials, today's consumers want to co-create. They want to be heard, seen and reflected in the brand's identity.

Platforms like Instagram, TikTok, and LinkedIn allow brands to celebrate customer stories. In turn, these authentic voices create layers of trust, community, and soulfulness that traditional ads can't replicate.

The future of marketing lies in this co-creation—where the brand and audience write the story together.

2. Understanding Your Audience's Needs Through Stories

a) *The Empathy Advantage*

Soulful content begins with empathy. It's not about what the brand wants to say but what the audience needs to hear. Through storytelling, marketers can mirror their audience's inner world—acknowledging their dreams, doubts, and daily realities.

Empathy fuels deeper audience insights. It encourages listening beyond demographics—getting into psychographics and emotional behaviour. For example, a tech-savvy Gen Z audience doesn't just want new gadgets—they seek content that addresses identity, purpose, and self-expression.

When content acknowledges those deeper needs, it moves from relevant to resonant.

b) Telling Stories that Reflect the Audience's Journey

The most impactful stories are not about the brand's heroism—they are about the customer's transformation. They say, "We see you. We understand what you're going through. Here's how we help you grow."

This approach is particularly relevant for service-based industries. Think of mental health apps, fitness programs, or online education platforms. Their content often revolves around real user stories—people who took a leap, experienced transformation, and reclaimed power in their lives.

Such stories create emotional validation, helping audiences feel heard and empowered. And when people feel seen, they engage—and they return.

c) Research-Driven Storytelling

Understanding your audience isn't guesswork—it requires listening, observing, and iterating. This is where data meets storytelling. Insights from search trends, social media comments, and user feedback offer invaluable clues.

For instance, a brand might discover that customers feel anxious about climate change. Rather than pitch eco-products directly, they could share real stories about communities and individuals making positive change. This values-based narrative goes deeper than product features—

it connects with the soul.

Brands that use data not just to personalize but to empathize create content that speaks the audience's language—and their emotional landscape.

3. Creating Relatable, Authentic Content

a) Ditching Perfection for Honesty

In the age of glossy influencer content and curated lives, what people crave most is realness. Authentic content—stories that show vulnerability, mistakes, and behind-the-scenes moments—outperforms polished ads because it builds credibility.

Authenticity doesn't mean unprofessionalism. It means being honest, being consistent, and being human. A founder sharing the brand's origin story, an employee talking about their first day, a customer review that includes the ups and downs—all of these bring texture and truth to the brand voice.

UK-based brands like Monzo and Gousto embrace this approach, openly discussing their growth challenges and customer feedback in their content. This transparency creates trust and relatability—two cornerstones of soulful content.

b) Reflecting Diverse Realities

A soulful brand doesn't speak to a single image of its audience—it speaks to the many. Representation matters. Today's audiences want to see people like them, hear stories like theirs, and feel that their truth is valid.

Whether it's race, gender identity, disability, neurodiversity, or cultural background, the content that includes and reflects these perspectives creates emotional safety and belonging.

One standout example is Channel 4's "Super. Human." campaign during the Paralympics, which powerfully showcased the stories of disabled athletes in a way that was bold, real, and inspiring. It wasn't about sympathy—it was about celebrating resilience. That's what speaking to the soul looks like.

c) *Making Content Personal and Purposeful*

Personalization is not just about inserting a name in an email—it's about delivering content that feels made for the individual. This means understanding where they are in their journey and crafting stories that support, inspire, or guide them.

At the same time, content must serve a larger purpose. People are increasingly aligning with brands that stand for something—social justice, sustainability, mental health, or education. A brand that uses its platform to tell stories that matter—not just to sell but to contribute—builds deep emotional equity.

In the UK, brands like Ben & Jerry's use their content to amplify social issues, showing how storytelling and activism can coexist powerfully.

Creating with Heart and Honesty

Content that speaks to the soul doesn't shout—it whispers. It doesn't persuade—it resonates. It doesn't sell—it connects. And in the creative economy, where trust is the new currency, that connection is everything.

We're living in a time where brands are publishers, creators, and community builders. To succeed, they must move beyond views, clicks, and conversions and focus on values, empathy, and storytelling. When a brand dares to be vulnerable, reflective, and human—it doesn't just win customers. It earns loyalists, advocates, and fans.

Creating soulful content isn't about the perfect post or viral moment. It's about consistency, honesty, and purpose. It's about meeting people, not just where they are—but who they are. That is the true power of storytelling in the modern marketing landscape.

Section 3: Case Studies of Successful Storytelling Campaigns

In today's ever-evolving world of marketing, storytelling has become more than just a strategy—it's the heart and soul of building authentic relationships with customers. But what does successful storytelling look like in action? How do real world campaigns take the narrative to the next level, generating emotion, loyalty, and measurable growth? Let's explore this together.

This section will take you on a journey through iconic global storytelling campaigns. We'll dig into how they've fostered deep brand loyalty and uncover the ways brands measure the true business impact of great stories. Through concrete case studies and strategic insights, we'll see how storytelling has moved from the edges of marketing to its very core.

1. Examples of Iconic Global Brand Stories

a) *Nike* – "Just Do It"

Nike's iconic slogan, *"Just Do It"*, is more than just a catchy line—it's the foundation of an emotional storytelling journey that's spanned decades. This isn't just about shoes. It's about the relentless human spirit, ambition, and defying the odds. Nike's campaigns have told the stories of athletes, dreamers, and even underdogs, always spotlighting courage, determination, and the relentless pursuit of greatness. Whether it's featuring disabled athletes or controversial figures like Colin Kaepernick, Nike's storytelling aligns with values that deeply resonate with their audience. It's not about selling shoes. It's about selling purpose, identity, and the feeling of empowerment.

Key takeaway: The best storytelling doesn't focus on the product—it highlights the values and emotions behind it.

b) *Dove* – "Real Beauty" Campaign

Back in 2004, Dove took a bold step that forever changed the beauty industry. Instead of relying on professional models, they featured real women of all sizes, shapes, and ethnicities. The stories shared in the campaign were raw, personal, and emotionally powerful. Dove's narrative highlighted the pressures of societal beauty standards, encouraging women to embrace their true selves. It wasn't just a marketing campaign—it was a social movement. By challenging these norms, Dove transformed from a personal care brand to a brand that advocates for self-esteem and body positivity.

The impact? Sales soared from $2.5 billion to $4 billion in just a year, and Dove became one of the most awarded brands in advertising history.

Key takeaway: When storytelling reflects your audience's truth, it transcends marketing. It becomes a cultural shift.

> c) *Apple* – "Shot on iPhone"

Apple's *"Shot on iPhone"* campaign is a brilliant example of user-generated storytelling. Instead of simply showcasing the phone's technical specs, Apple highlighted real photos and videos taken by everyday iPhone users. The stories behind these images—ordinary people capturing extraordinary moments—spoke volumes. Whether it was a family on vacation, a couple's first dance, or a breathtaking landscape, Apple let its customers tell the story.

Key takeaway: Empowering your audience to share their own stories deepens emotional connections and fosters authenticity.

> d) *John Lewis* – Christmas Ad Series *(UK)*

Every year, the UK eagerly awaits John Lewis's Christmas adverts. These short films, though almost entirely devoid of product placement, tug at the heartstrings of millions. Whether it's a lonely man on the moon or a child nurturing a dragon, emotional storytelling doesn't just sell products—it creates a moment of magic, an emotional connection. These ads have become a staple of Christmas culture, evoking emotions of family, love, and togetherness.

Key takeaway: Emotional storytelling, when tied to cultural moments or seasonal rituals, can become an iconic part of public culture.

e) *Airbnb* – "Belong Anywhere"

At its core, Airbnb isn't just about booking rooms—it's about belonging. The brand's narrative revolves around the idea of human connection. Whether it's a solo traveller finding kindness in a foreign country or a family opening their doors to strangers, Airbnb's campaigns celebrate stories of shared experiences and global connections. The brand tells personal stories through documentary-style content, social media campaigns, and user testimonials, making each customer a chapter in its ongoing narrative.

Key takeaway: Great storytelling creates a shared identity—a community customers are proud to be a part of.

2. How Storytelling Drives Brand Loyalty

a) *Emotional Bonds Build Long-Term Relationships*

Think about the brands that have stood by you through thick and thin. Why are you loyal to them? Chances are, it's not because of a discount you once received. It's because their story has touched your heart. Stories create deep emotional bonds, and when you see yourself reflected in a brand's narrative, loyalty becomes a natural extension of that connection.

A Nike customer doesn't just wear a shoe—they wear a belief. A Dove customer isn't just buying soap—they're investing in a movement that celebrates authenticity. These emotional connections don't just fade away after a single purchase; they build a lasting, meaningful relationship.

b) *Storytelling Reinforces Brand Values*

Every story a brand tells reinforces its core values. When a brand's values align with your own, loyalty becomes more than just a transaction—it becomes part of your identity. Think of Patagonia. Their storytelling doesn't just promote outdoor gear; it champions environmental activism. Customers are not just purchasing products; they're supporting a company whose mission they believe in.

c) Stories Create Memories, Not Just Messages

You'll remember a brand's story long after the ad has ended. Why? Because stories live in your heart, not just your mind. They evoke emotions that stick with you, becoming memories that shape your future choices. A well-told story isn't just forgotten—it becomes part of your narrative, and that emotional recall increases brand loyalty. Think back to brands that made you feel something during the pandemic. Those brands who shared stories of hope and community support saw stronger engagement than those who didn't.

d) Shared Narratives Foster Community

Storytelling doesn't just create individual loyalty—it fosters a community of like-minded individuals who share the same values and beliefs. When audiences engage with a brand's story, they become part of a collective identity. Brands like LEGO and Glossier have excelled at empowering their fans to tell their own stories. This approach builds a community that feels connected, valued, and heard.

3. Measuring the Impact of Storytelling on Brand Success

a) Beyond Clicks: Defining Storytelling KPIs

Storytelling is emotional, but its impact can and should be measured. However, the metrics are different from traditional performance marketing. Rather than focusing on immediate conversions, we should be looking at awareness, engagement, sentiment, and loyalty. Here are some KPIs that measure how deeply a story resonates:

- Brand recall (both unaided and aided)

- Time spent with content

- Emotional response (through biometric tools or sentiment analysis)

- Social sharing and virality

- Repeat purchase rates

- Net Promoter Score (NPS)

These metrics help us understand not just how many people saw the story but how much it moved them.

b) Sentiment Analysis and Social Listening

Tools like Brandwatch, Sprinklr, and Talkwalker help brands track conversations around their campaigns. Are people reacting emotionally? What themes are emerging? By analyzing sentiment, brands can pinpoint the aspects of the story that resonated most. This can guide future campaigns and content strategies.

c) First-Party Data and CRM Insights

By analyzing customer behaviour within CRM systems, brands can see how storytelling impacts loyalty and purchasing habits. Are customers who engage with the brand's story more likely to return? Do they spend more or advocate for the brand? These insights offer solid data to assess the long-term impact of storytelling.

d) Case Study: John Lewis Christmas Ad ROI

John Lewis has shown that storytelling doesn't just build emotional connections— it drives tangible results. In 2011, their *"The Long Wait"* Christmas ad led to a 9.3% increase in sales over the holiday period. Even without directly pushing products, their storytelling created a lasting emotional impact that drove foot traffic and sales.

e) The Long-Term Brand Equity Effect

Storytelling isn't just for short-term results—it's an investment in long-term brand equity. Over time, it shapes how the world sees your brand. Brands like Apple, Nike, and Google have stayed on top for decades because of the stories they tell. These stories build trust, relevance, and a deep emotional connection that keeps customers loyal, even when mistakes are made, or competitors offer a better deal.

Stories That Shape Strategy and Success

Let's pause for a moment and think about the power of stories. Really think about it. The stories we tell aren't just for entertainment or passing the time. They're much more than that. They're tools that shape who we are, how we connect with each other, and—most importantly—how we build and communicate our brands.

As we've explored through the case studies of some of the world's most iconic brands, storytelling has proven time and time again to be far more than just a marketing tactic. It's a fundamental strategy that can define a brand's identity, foster unbreakable loyalty, and ultimately drive long-term success.

When you think about brands like Nike, Dove, and John Lewis, what comes to mind? It's not just the products they sell, is it? It's the stories they've woven into the fabric of their campaigns. Nike doesn't just sell athletic wear; they sell empowerment. They tell stories of overcoming adversity, pushing boundaries, and achieving greatness. Each ad, each campaign, is a chapter in the larger story they tell about strength, determination, and resilience. That's what makes Nike more than a brand—it makes them a symbol, a movement.

And then there's Dove. Dove's approach isn't just about soap or shampoo; it's about authenticity, real beauty, and self-love. In a world where we're often bombarded with unattainable beauty standards, Dove chose to tell a different kind of story. They gave voice to real women with real bodies, real faces, and real stories to tell. Through their "Real Beauty" campaign, Dove reshaped what it meant to be beautiful in a way that resonated deeply with millions of people around the world. It wasn't just about selling products; it was about changing perceptions, sparking important conversations, and making people feel seen, heard, and valued.

And let's not forget John Lewis, whose annual holiday commercials have become almost as anticipated as the holiday season itself. These commercials aren't just about shopping; they're about creating magic, about connecting with the deepest parts of our humanity—the parts that crave kindness, connection, and joy. John Lewis has turned their Christmas campaigns into a tradition that brings people together, stirs emotions, and builds anticipation for what's to come. They understand that the holidays aren't just about presents—they're about the stories we share, the emotions we feel, and the moments that stay with us long after the decorations are packed away.

So, what's the common thread between all of these brands? It's simple: stories. These companies have figured out how to turn storytelling into something far greater than a marketing tool. It's their strategy. It's what gives their brands a heartbeat, a soul. Stories are the bedrock upon which they've built their identities, and it's through these stories that they've cultivated loyalty, inspired trust, and achieved incredible growth.

Now, why does this matter to you? Because, in today's world, stories are more valuable than ever. We live in a time where attention is a rare commodity, and trust is even rarer. People are bombarded with thousands of messages every single day, and it's easy to become numb to the noise. But stories? Stories cut through the clutter. They resonate. They stick with us long after the details have faded. When done right, they create a connection that goes beyond a product or service. They build relationships. They create communities. And when those stories are authentic, they create legacies.

This is the power of storytelling—it gives brands their soul. It's the secret to shaping a brand's future. If you want to differentiate yourself in a crowded marketplace, you need to have a story that's worth telling. A story that's compelling, relatable, and rooted in authenticity. You can't just be another voice in the crowd; you need to be the voice that people listen to, the one they remember, the one they trust.

So, what's the lesson here? It's simple: If you want to shape your brand's future, start by telling stories that are worth remembering. Don't just sell a product—sell a story that people can connect with, a story that reflects who you are, what you stand for, and why you matter. Because, in the end, it's not just the products that we remember. It's the stories that stick with us long after the sale is made.

And that, my friend, is how you create something lasting—something that transcends time, trends, and transactions. Something that truly shapes your brand's identity and leads to success. So, go ahead. Tell your story. Make it unforgettable. Make it meaningful. And watch as it becomes the foundation of everything you build.

Chapter 6
Creative Technology and Innovation

We've come a long way, haven't we? When I look back, I'm amazed at how quickly things have changed. Just a few decades ago, the divide between creativity and technology seemed so clear-cut, so rigid. On one side, you had the **engineers**, the ones who could code, build, and engineer the future. On the other, you had the **artists**, the dreamers and the creators who painted the world with imagination and emotion. But today? That line has blurred so completely it's almost impossible to tell where one ends and the other begins.

What was once considered separate territories has now merged into something far more exciting and far more **powerful**. Now, technology isn't just a support system for creativity—it's the fuel that **amplifies** it. It pushes boundaries in ways we could never have imagined before. It challenges what we thought was possible and opens doors to experiences that were once the stuff of dreams. And as this fusion of creativity and technology continues to evolve, it's transforming not just how we create but how we **connect** with the world.

Think about it: **brands** are no longer limited by what was once possible. They're venturing into **new frontiers**, reaching wider audiences, and creating experiences that are more immersive and impactful than ever before. They're pushing the envelope in ways that make you stop and say, "How did they do that?" and "Why didn't I think of that?" Whether it's a brand launching a **virtual reality experience** or using **AI-powered ads** that seem to know you better than your best friend, we're living in a time where the creative possibilities are limitless.

In this section, we're going to dive into how technology is reshaping the creative world. We'll explore the ways in which **brands** are harnessing the power of **artificial intelligence (AI)** and **automation** to **elevate** their marketing efforts. These tools aren't just about making things faster—they're about making things **smarter**. AI is helping brands understand consumer behaviour on a level that was once unfathomable. It's allowing them to anticipate needs, create highly personalized experiences, and engage with audiences in ways that feel almost **human**. Automation, on the other hand, is freeing up time for creativity to flourish. It's enabling brands to focus on what they do best— **innovating, connecting,** and **inspiring**.

And then there's **data**. Data is no longer just a buzzword. It's the backbone of everything. It's the foundation upon which **creative decisions** are made. Through data, brands can get a clearer picture of what's working, what's not, and what their audience truly craves. No longer do we have to rely on guesswork or intuition alone; data gives us the tools to be more precise, more effective, and ultimately more **successful** in our creative endeavours.

This is the beauty of the world we live in today: creativity and technology are no longer separate entities. They're partners, working side by side to shape the future of marketing and beyond. And the result? A whole new world of creative possibilities that we get to explore together. So, let's take a deeper dive into this fusion and discover how it's changing everything.

The Fusion of Technology and Creativity

1. How Technology is Changing the Creative Landscape

a) *The Digital Revolution in Creativity*

Think about it: just a few decades ago, if you wanted to create, you had to rely on traditional tools like paint, paper, film, or physical cameras. Fast forward to today, and the possibilities seem endless. Thanks to the digital revolution, creativity has been freed from its old constraints. Now, we have sophisticated software, platforms, and tools that marry human imagination with the raw power of computing. The world of creativity has evolved with the rise of digital tools like graphic design software, video editing programs, and 3D modelling tools. Artists, marketers, and creators can now manifest their ideas in ways they could only dream of before.

Take programs like Adobe Creative Cloud, Final Cut Pro, or Cinema 4D— combined with powerful computers and user-friendly design capabilities—they allow us to create in more detailed, immersive, and technically advanced ways. But it doesn't stop there. The emergence of virtual reality (VR) and augmented reality (AR) has opened entirely new realms of interactive storytelling, giving consumers an entirely fresh way to connect with brands.

And then, there's social media. We can't ignore the impact it's had. Platforms like Instagram, TikTok, YouTube, and Pinterest have transformed creativity from a reserved skill to something everyone can access. These platforms have made creativity more democratic, where anyone with a camera and a vision can share their work with the world. It's no longer just about content consumption—it's about participating in creative collaboration, where trends and challenges spark global conversations.

b) Technology Expanding Creative Expression

Technology is giving creators new ways to express themselves, and it's a game-changer. Think about musicians, filmmakers, photographers, and graphic designers who now have the freedom to create, share, and even monetize their work on global platforms like Spotify, YouTube, Vimeo, and Adobe Spark. The opportunities for creative expression have become more inclusive and more diverse.

Take, for example, the rise of generative art. Algorithms are now helping artists create visual masterpieces or music in ways that were once the realm of human imagination alone. Platforms like Runway ML or DeepArt use machine learning to help artists interpret data, textures, and styles in unique, innovative ways that would have been impossible in the past.

And when it comes to marketing, new tech tools—like chatbots, virtual assistants, and immersive web experiences—are transforming how brands connect with their audiences. These technologies don't just talk at the customer; they converse, they respond, and they evolve based on interactions. It's like having a meaningful conversation with a brand rather than just being spoken to. It's a dynamic relationship that builds deeper emotional connections.

2. Leveraging AI and Automation in Creative Marketing

a) *Artificial Intelligence and Creativity*

AI is revolutionizing the marketing landscape in ways we couldn't have predicted. While AI is known for data analytics and machine learning, it's now entering the creative arena. It's helping marketers generate personalized experiences, create engaging content, and automate tasks that used to take up time and energy.

Consider AI-generated content: platforms like Copy.ai or Jasper AI enable marketers to generate text for blogs, emails, ads, and social media posts in a fraction of the time. Using natural language processing (NLP), these tools generate human-like text based on a few key prompts. Now, marketers can focus on the big picture—strategy creativity—while AI handles the grunt work.

AI is also making waves in image and video creation. Tools like DeepAI and Runway ML can generate visuals or videos just from a written prompt. Think about how much faster brands can now generate custom visual content on demand and how much more personal and dynamic that content can be.

And let's not forget video production. AI-driven video editing tools like Magisto or Pictory automatically adjust content, choosing the right transitions, filters, and audio to match the video's message. These tools make the process faster while ensuring the content stays relevant and impactful. It's AI making creativity both efficient and effective.

b) *Automation in Creative Marketing*

Automation has truly transformed how brands connect with their audiences. It streamlines routine tasks like sending emails, scheduling social media posts, and segmenting customers based on behaviour. What does this mean for marketers? It means more time to focus on strategy and creativity—on the things that really matter.

And it's not just about automating tasks. Creative automation is gaining traction. Dynamic ads are an excellent example. With machine learning, brands can automatically adjust creative elements—like visuals and text—based on user preferences and behaviour. Think Google Ads or Facebook Ads, where creative elements change to target specific audience segments.

Automation is also taking customer engagement to a whole new level. AI-driven chatbots don't just respond to queries—they personalize the experience. From answering questions in real time to guiding customers through the purchasing process and recommending products based on previous behaviour, these bots are enhancing how we engage with brands.

3. The Role of Data in Creative Decision-Making

a) Data-Driven Creativity

Creativity used to be about gut feeling, instinct, and emotion. Today, data is just as important. With the right tools, marketers no longer have to guess what will work— they can predict it. Data-driven creativity allows marketers to analyze consumer behaviour, engagement patterns, and preferences to craft tailored campaigns that hit the mark.

Tools like Google Analytics, HubSpot, and Tableau offer insights into which creative elements resonate most with your audience. Engagement metrics like click-through rates, shares, and comments give marketers the data they need to tweak content strategies for maximum impact.

b) A/B Testing and Iterative Creativity

One of the most powerful tools in a data-driven creative toolkit is A/B testing. Testing different versions of content allows marketers to see which resonates most with their audience. Whether it's testing different colours, headlines, or video lengths, A/B testing enables continuous improvement—making sure that every decision is backed by data, not guesswork.

c) Predictive Analytics in Creative Strategy

Predictive analytics takes data-driven creativity to the next level. By analyzing historical data and using algorithms to predict future trends and outcomes, marketers can anticipate consumer needs and behaviours. This allows them to design campaigns that are in tune with upcoming trends, ensuring they're one step ahead of the curve.

d) Balancing Data and Creativity

Here's the thing—data is invaluable, but it's not the whole story. Creativity still requires intuition, emotion, and a spark of magic. It's about finding the balance between data and creativity, using data to guide decisions but not replace the human element that makes creative work special.

The fusion of technology and creativity is transforming the marketing landscape into something dynamic and exciting. Technology has unlocked so many new possibilities—from AI-generated content to creative automation and data-driven decision-making. As we embrace an increasingly digital world, the key to successful marketing is understanding how to balance cutting-edge technology with the heart of creativity. In the end, it's this fusion that will allow brands to craft meaningful, unforgettable experiences.

In the next section, we'll dive deeper into creative innovation, exploring how brands continue to reinvent themselves to stay relevant in an ever-evolving technological landscape.

Innovation in Digital Marketing

The world of digital marketing is shifting before our eyes, changing in ways we couldn't have imagined a few years ago. It's all thanks to rapid technological advancements that allow brands to connect with their customers in deeply personalized and dynamic ways. What used to work in the past—the old, tried-and-true marketing strategies—just doesn't cut it anymore. To truly make an impact in today's market, brands have to embrace innovation. They need to stand out, make lasting connections, and, most importantly, stay relevant to their audience. In this section, I'll take you through three incredible innovations in digital marketing: Virtual Reality (VR) and Augmented Reality (AR), Predictive Analytics, and Interactive Content. These powerful tools are completely changing how brands communicate, engage, and build loyalty with their customers.

1. Virtual Reality and Augmented Reality in Marketing

a) Defining VR and AR in Marketing

Virtual Reality (VR) and Augmented Reality (AR)—these aren't just some sci-fi buzzwords anymore. They're here, and they're revolutionizing how brands market their products. VR and AR are immersive technologies that allow users to interact with digital elements in real time. They're creating experiences that were once beyond our wildest imagination.

- **Virtual Reality (VR)** takes us into a fully digital environment, immersing us in a completely virtual world. Think about VR headsets like the Oculus Rift or HTC Vive—they can transport you into a virtual store, giving you a chance to experience a brand or product like never before.

- **Augmented Reality (AR)**, however, overlays digital content onto the real world. You don't need a headset for this; all you need is your smartphone, tablet, or even special AR glasses. AR is all about enhancing the world you already know, bringing digital elements into it in meaningful ways.

Both VR and AR are becoming the ultimate tools in any marketer's toolbox, offering consumers experiences that go beyond the ordinary, sparking deeper interactions and engagement.

b) How VR and AR are Transforming Marketing

The way VR and AR are changing marketing is nothing short of revolutionary. These technologies are opening up new, immersive ways to discover products, and they're even shaping customer loyalty.

For example, VR allows potential buyers to step inside a property and take a virtual tour of homes, no matter where they are in the world. It's incredible for real estate marketing, and the convenience of it all makes the experience even more magical.

Then there's AR. This tech is way more accessible, offering consumers the ability to try products in their own space before committing to a purchase. Take IKEA's AR app, for instance. It lets users place virtual furniture in their own living rooms, helping them see how the pieces fit and look. This is more than just convenience— it's a game-changer. It reduces the likelihood of returns and allows customers to be more confident in their decisions.

c) Enhancing Customer Engagement through Immersive Experiences

The beauty of VR and AR lies in their ability to create unforgettable experiences. Research shows that consumers who engage with these technologies are far more likely to develop a strong emotional connection to the brand, resulting in increased loyalty and sales.

Brands are using this to their advantage. Nike, for example, has integrated AR into its retail experience. Imagine walking into a store, scanning a pair of shoes with your phone, and then instantly accessing detailed product info, customer reviews, and customization options. It's not just a shopping experience; it's an interactive journey that builds trust and provides value. Plus, AR-driven fun experiences— like Snapchat's AR filters—engage customers in creative, lighthearted ways, which only strengthens the emotional ties with the brand.

2. The Power of Predictive Analytics for Marketing Campaigns

a) Defining Predictive Analytics

Let me tell you, predictive analytics is a game-changer for marketers. It's like having a crystal ball that lets you peek into the future. This advanced data analysis combines machine learning, statistical algorithms, and historical data to predict future outcomes. In marketing, it allows brands to anticipate customer behaviour and tailor their strategies before the consumer even knows what they want.

By analyzing past data—like sales history, customer interactions, browsing patterns, and demographics—predictive analytics reveals hidden trends that can drive smarter decision-making. It helps marketers understand who's likely to convert, what type of content will resonate, and the perfect timing for a campaign.

b) How Predictive Analytics Enhances Marketing Campaigns

What's amazing about predictive analytics is that it increases both efficiency and ROI. Imagine knowing which products will be in demand next season. With predictive insights, brands can plan inventory and marketing efforts months ahead of time, ensuring they hit the ground running.

It also plays a massive role in customer segmentation. By understanding what different customer groups value, marketers can craft targeted campaigns that speak directly to their needs. Let's say an online store uses predictive analytics to identify shoppers who are likely to make repeat purchases—they can then send them personalized offers, increasing the chance of conversion.

Moreover, predictive analytics boosts ad targeting. With platforms like Google Ads and Facebook Ads, predictive analytics helps brands deliver hyper-targeted ads to the right audience at the right time, ensuring the maximum return for every dollar spent.

c) The Role of AI in Predictive Analytics

Artificial Intelligence (AI) is the secret weapon in predictive analytics. It automates data processing at lightning speed and uncovers patterns that would be impossible to spot with the human eye. This means marketers get real-time insights, allowing them to make decisions quickly and efficiently.

Imagine AI algorithms analyzing a customer's purchase history, website visits, and social media interactions to predict what they're most likely to buy next. With that kind of power, marketers can craft personalized campaigns that feel like they were designed just for one person. The result? Higher engagement and more conversions.

3. How Interactive Content is Shaping Customer Engagement

a) Defining Interactive Content

Interactive content is shaking up the digital marketing world. Unlike traditional content, which you simply consume, interactive content invites you to engage. Whether it's through quizzes, polls, surveys, interactive videos, or even calculators, it makes you an active participant in the experience.

Interactive content is a powerful tool that marketers can use to offer personalized experiences while gathering valuable insights into customer preferences. When customers interact with content, they feel more connected to the brand. This connection fosters loyalty, increases engagement, and ultimately drives conversions.

b) The Benefits of Interactive Content in Marketing

Why is interactive content such a big deal? For one, it significantly boosts engagement. People love participating, whether it's taking a quiz to find their ideal product or watching an interactive video that allows them to choose their own path. The more involved users get, the more they connect with the brand.

A great example is BuzzFeed's personality quizzes or Spotify's "Wrapped" campaign, which invites users to relive their year in music. These experiences are interactive by design, and they encourage users to share their results with friends and followers, amplifying brand awareness and deepening customer engagement.

Interactive content also helps brands collect crucial data. By analyzing how users interact with elements like quizzes or calculators, marketers gain deep insights into their audience's preferences and behaviours. This data can then be used to create even more targeted, personalized content.

c) Enhancing Customer Experience with Interactive Content

Interactive content doesn't just increase engagement—it also enhances the customer experience by adding value. Take Sephora's Virtual Artist, for instance. It lets customers try on makeup virtually through AR. This isn't just a fun gimmick; it actually helps consumers make purchase decisions while enhancing their overall shopping experience. They feel more confident in their choices, and they have a memorable experience while doing it.

Interactive content also helps guide consumers through the decision-making process. Whether it's an interactive product demo or a customized quiz, it helps customers explore and understand a product's value before making a purchase.

What's more, it encourages sharing and virality. Users who engage with interactive content are more likely to share their experience with their network, extending a brand's reach and credibility.

Innovation in digital marketing is reshaping the way brands connect with their customers. From the immersive worlds created by VR and AR to the data-driven insights offered by predictive analytics and the personal touch of interactive content, the digital marketing landscape is filled with endless possibilities. These innovations aren't just making marketing smarter—they're helping brands create stronger, more meaningful relationships with their customers. As we continue to evolve in this digital age, the brands that succeed will be those that embrace innovation, stay agile, and continuously engage their customers in ways that truly matter.

The Future of Creative Technologies

The world of marketing is on the brink of something truly revolutionary. New technologies are reshaping how we create, connect, and communicate, giving us exciting new ways to engage with consumers. As technology continues to evolve at an incredible pace, marketers like you and me need to stay ahead of the curve, ready to embrace these innovations and keep up in this fast-moving global marketplace. In this section, I'll share three game-changing technologies that are shaping the future of creative marketing: Artificial Intelligence (AI), Blockchain, and Ethical Considerations in Creative Technology.

These technologies aren't just transforming how content is created and marketed; they're also raising the bar for transparency, security, and ethical responsibility in the digital world. So, let's dive deeper into each of these forces and explore how they're changing the landscape for the creative industries.

1. How AI is Transforming Content Creation

Artificial Intelligence (AI) isn't some distant dream anymore—it's a powerful tool that marketers are using right now to enhance creativity, improve efficiency, and save time. We often think of AI as something futuristic, something that might only be seen in sci-fi movies. But in reality, AI is already here, and it's playing a significant role in shaping the world of content creation in ways we never thought possible.

Let me ask you: Have you ever felt overwhelmed by the constant pressure to create fresh, engaging content day after day? You're not alone. The world of marketing has always been driven by the need for **new ideas, new stories**, and **new ways to connect** with audiences. The challenge lies in creating that content quickly and consistently—without burning out. Enter AI, which has become a game-changer for marketers everywhere.

AI isn't here to replace human creativity. Far from it. What AI does is **amplify** it. By automating repetitive tasks and providing data-driven insights, AI frees up valuable time for creatives to focus on what really matters—bringing their **ideas to life**. Imagine having a tool that can sift through mountains of data in seconds, analyze trends, and suggest personalized content strategies based on real-time information. Sounds pretty amazing, right? That's the power of AI.

Let's break it down a little more. When it comes to **content creation,**

AI is making a real impact. Take **content generation** tools, for instance. AI-powered platforms can now generate copy for blogs, social media posts, and even advertisements in a fraction of the time it would take a human. While these tools still need that human touch to ensure the content is emotional, engaging, and authentic, they provide a solid foundation, taking over tasks like **SEO optimization, data analysis**, and even **content curation**.

But AI goes beyond just **speed**—it brings a new level of **personalization**. By analyzing **consumer behaviour**, AI can help create content that resonates with the specific preferences of your target audience. It can predict what kind of content will catch their attention, when to post it, and how to phrase it in a way that truly speaks to them. So, the next time you sit down to create a post or write an email campaign, imagine having a tool that knows your audience's desires almost as well as you do. That's where AI comes in.

Then, there's the aspect of **efficiency**. Content creation doesn't just involve coming up with ideas—it also involves fine-tuning, editing, and optimizing. AI can help with all of that. It can suggest edits, recommend headline options, and even point out areas where the copy could be improved based on audience engagement metrics. For marketers, this means more time to focus on strategy and creative direction while leaving the heavy lifting to AI.

And it doesn't stop there. AI is also helping with **visual content creation**. Imagine using AI to generate custom images or video edits based on a brief or template. The technology is now sophisticated enough to create visuals that match the tone, style, and emotion of the content you want to convey. Whether it's **Instagram posts**, **promotional videos**, or even **interactive content**, AI can help bring your vision to life in ways that were once only possible with extensive resources or an entire team of designers.

But here's the most beautiful thing about AI in content creation: it **learns**. The more it interacts with data, the better it becomes at predicting what works and what doesn't. It starts with understanding your audience's preferences, allowing you to create more targeted and impactful content over time. This means that AI isn't just a tool that does the job—it's a partner that **evolves with you**. It helps you stay on top of trends, adapt to changes, and remain relevant in a fast-paced, ever-changing digital landscape.

So, let's be clear: AI is not just an assistant in content creation—it's a catalyst for innovation. It's a tool that can help you move faster, work smarter, and create content that truly speaks to your audience. It amplifies your creativity, giving you the freedom to push boundaries, explore new ideas, and take risks. And in today's world of marketing, that's what we need more than ever—innovation and the ability to adapt.

As we move into the future, AI will continue to shape the way we approach content creation. But remember—AI can only go so far. The magic still lies in the hands of human creators who know how to blend **data-driven insights** with **authenticity**, **empathy**, and a **deep understanding of their audience**. Together, AI and human creativity will create a perfect synergy that will define the future of marketing.

a) *AI-Powered Content Generation*

One of the most mind-blowing ways AI is transforming content creation is through automated content generation. Imagine this: AI algorithms that can write articles, generate social media posts, and even craft personalized email content. For instance, tools like GPT-3 (yes, the very model you're reading right now) can produce human-like text based on simple prompts. This ability to create high-quality, relevant content on demand is changing the game for businesses everywhere.

But it doesn't stop at text. AI is also revolutionizing the creation of visual content. Tools like Canva and Adobe Sensei are using AI to help users quickly generate design layouts, choose colour schemes, and even create social media posts with minimal effort. This frees up time for businesses to focus on more complex creative strategies while AI handles repetitive tasks.

b) *Personalization Through AI*

One of the coolest things about AI is its ability to enable hyper-personalization in marketing. This isn't just about making content relevant—it's about tailoring experiences to each individual user's needs and desires. Think about how Netflix suggests movies based on your past choices or how Spotify creates personalized playlists just for you. That's AI at work.

Marketers are increasingly using AI to create personalized email campaigns, web content, and digital ads based on user data. And because AI continuously learns from every user interaction, it helps businesses keep customers engaged. As AI evolves, expect even more sophisticated forms of personalization where every touchpoint with a brand feels like it was created just for you.

c) AI in Video Content Creation

Let's talk about video—because we all know that video content is one of the most engaging ways to reach people. And yes, AI is making waves here, too. Imagine AI tools that can automatically edit and produce video content—tasks that used to take hours now get done in a fraction of the time. AI can even summarize videos, add subtitles, and suggest the best clips based on the script.

But that's not all. AI is helping create interactive videos where viewers can choose their own narrative paths or engage with the content in real time. This level of interaction isn't just new; it's game-changing for video marketing, offering brands fresh, innovative ways to connect with their audience.

2. The Role of Blockchain in Marketing and Brand Transparency

Blockchain is a term we've all heard, mostly tied to cryptocurrencies like Bitcoin. But did you know that it's making its way into marketing? Blockchain offers some incredible benefits when it comes to transparency, security, and building trust with your audience— something that's more crucial than ever as consumers become more aware of data privacy issues. Let's explore how blockchain is changing the marketing game.

a) Enhancing Transparency and Trust

Blockchain's decentralized nature means that data can't be altered or manipulated by a single party. This is huge when it comes to building transparency in marketing. Consumers are savvy, and they're increasingly looking for brands that prioritize honesty and transparency. With blockchain, you can offer an immutable record of transactions, allowing customers to trace a product's journey from creation to purchase.

Take IBM's Food Trust blockchain network, for example. This allows consumers to track the origin of their food products, ensuring they come from ethical, sustainable sources. Similarly, blockchain is being used in advertising to track ad impressions, ensuring that advertisers only pay for legitimate views and clicks.

b) Blockchain for Digital Advertising

Digital advertising has long struggled with issues like fraud, data privacy, and inefficiency. Blockchain can help tackle these problems head-on. By using blockchain, advertisers can track the entire process of ad distribution, ensuring that each step is secure and transparent. This helps eliminate ad fraud, ensuring advertisers only pay for real impressions and views.

Moreover, blockchain also puts consumers in control of their own data. With privacy laws like the GDPR gaining traction, consumers are more aware of how their personal data is being used. Blockchain allows users to control who has access to their information, and they can even get compensated for sharing their data. This creates a more ethical and transparent advertising ecosystem.

c) Cryptocurrency in Brand Loyalty and Rewards

Blockchain isn't just about transparency and security—it's also creating new opportunities for brand loyalty and rewards. With cryptocurrency-based loyalty programs, brands can offer customers digital rewards or tokens that they can redeem for goods or services or even convert to other forms of cryptocurrency. This opens up a whole new world of possibilities for engaging customers and rewarding them in meaningful ways.

Blockchain-based loyalty programs, like LoyaltyLion, are secure, transparent, and tradable, giving customers a sense of ownership and value. These systems can help foster deeper brand loyalty by providing rewards that are more tangible and meaningful to tech-savvy consumers.

3. Ethical Considerations in Creative Technology

As marketers, we have a responsibility to use these powerful technologies ethically. While AI, blockchain, and other creative technologies offer incredible potential, they also come with ethical challenges that we must navigate with care. The future of creative marketing isn't just about innovation—it's also about doing the right thing.

a) *Data Privacy and Consumer Rights*

One of the most pressing ethical concerns in digital marketing is data privacy. With AI and blockchain collecting, analyzing, and storing vast amounts of personal data, we need to ensure that we're respecting consumers' privacy. Blockchain, however, offers a solution by allowing users to control who has access to their data and what it's used for. This is a step toward greater transparency and trust in the marketing world.

b) *AI Ethics and Bias in Content Creation*

Another challenge is the risk of bias in AI-generated content. AI is only as good as the data it's trained on, and if those datasets are biased, the content it produces could be, too. This could lead to reinforcing stereotypes or excluding diverse perspectives. Marketers need to be vigilant in ensuring that AI-generated content is inclusive, accurate, and free from harmful biases.

c) *Sustainability and Ethical Marketing*

Finally, we need to consider the environmental and social impact of the technologies we use. AI and blockchain, while powerful, require significant computational power, which can contribute to energy consumption. As marketers, we need to use these technologies responsibly, ensuring that our strategies promote sustainability and align with ethical consumer values.

The future of creative technologies in marketing is incredibly exciting. AI, blockchain, and other innovations are revolutionizing how we create and connect with consumers. These technologies promise to make marketing more personalized, transparent, and efficient—but we must approach them with care and responsibility. By embracing these technologies while considering the ethical implications, we can create marketing strategies that not only drive business success but also build trust and loyalty with our audiences.

As we continue on this journey of technological evolution, the possibilities for how we connect with customers are endless. The future is now, and it's up to us to shape it responsibly and creatively.

Chapter 7
Leading with a Creative Mindset

Leadership in marketing isn't what it used to be. In fact, if you've been in the industry for any length of time, you've probably already noticed that the rules are constantly being rewritten. Over the years, industries have evolved, and so too have the expectations placed on those in leadership positions. What was once a straightforward path—where leaders had their set ways of doing things—has now been replaced with an unpredictable landscape that demands flexibility, innovation, and, above all, **creativity**.

I'm sure you've seen it. The marketing world moves at lightning speed. One minute, a strategy that seemed cutting-edge is suddenly outdated. The next minute, a new trend or technology shifts the conversation entirely. It's an environment where change isn't just common—it's constant. And if you're still clinging to traditional leadership models, it's easy to feel like you're chasing the waves rather than riding them.

So, what does this mean for us? It means that we, as leaders, need to rethink how we approach leadership, especially within the creative domain. Gone are the days when decisions came solely from the top down, neatly packaged in a hierarchical structure. Today, we're seeing something new, something more dynamic. It's a shift towards leaders who are not only adaptable but **forward-thinking**, **collaborative**, and, above all, **creative**. These leaders aren't simply trying to keep up with change—they're actively shaping it.

Think about the leaders you admire in the marketing world. Chances are, they're not the ones holding onto the old ways of doing things. They're the ones who have embraced flexibility, who trust their teams to innovate, and who make room for bold ideas to emerge. The best leaders today are the ones who create spaces where creativity thrives, where experimentation is encouraged, and where the team feels supported in exploring new approaches. They are the ones who understand that **creativity is not just an asset but a necessity** in today's marketing landscape.

But what exactly makes creative leadership so essential today? Well, it's the difference between merely surviving in a fast-moving industry and truly **thriving** in it. Creative leadership fuels the kind of innovation that pushes boundaries and captivates audiences. It's about leading with vision, yes, but also about encouraging others to think differently, take risks, and bring fresh ideas to the table. Creative leaders understand that the best ideas often come from unexpected places—so they give space for everyone to contribute, not just the top brass.

This shift towards creative leadership is not just about changing how we manage teams—it's about changing how we think about the very role of a leader in marketing. It's no longer enough to have the answers. A great leader today knows how to ask the right questions, how to inspire those around them to dream bigger, and how to harness creativity in ways that drive **real, meaningful change**.

In today's world, leadership in marketing means **empowering others to create**— not just following a script but writing one that hasn't been written yet. And that, my friends, is the essence of creative leadership: a vision that embraces change, that challenges the status quo, and that drives progress in ways we never imagined possible. So, if we're going to lead in this new era, we have to be ready to change the game— together.

The Evolution of Leadership in Marketing

1. How Creative Leadership is Different from Traditional Leadership

Let's take a moment to think about the traditional leadership models that have dominated industries for so long. These models were based on a command-and-control system, where leaders were the decision-makers, the ones with all the answers. The hierarchy was clear—leaders made the decisions, and employees followed them. Efficiency, stability, and short-term goals were the focus. And while this worked in certain environments, in the fast-paced marketing world, this approach simply isn't enough.

Creative leadership, however, is different. It's all about fostering innovation, empowering teams, and encouraging collaboration. As a creative leader, you're not just executing strategies—you're creating an environment where creativity can flourish. This means you're encouraging risk-taking, experimentation, and thinking outside the box— qualities that are essential for marketing success in the digital age.

a) Empowering Creativity Over Commanding Compliance

Think about it: traditional leaders often viewed creativity as something "nice to have," reserved for the marketing or design teams. But creative leaders—well, they understand that creativity isn't just a nice extra—it's vital for everything. Whether you're creating a marketing campaign, designing a customer experience, or solving a problem within your team, creativity is the heartbeat of all business functions.

Creative leaders don't simply manage; they empower. They give their teams the resources, the tools, and the freedom to think boldly and take risks. They don't dictate the solutions—they create a space for their teams to explore new ideas where innovation and creativity can truly shine. By doing this, they unlock the full potential of their teams and allow them to achieve breakthroughs that lead to real growth.

b) Embracing Collaboration and Cross-Disciplinary Teams

I'm sure you've seen it: in traditional leadership models, departments often operate in silos. Marketing, sales, and product development—each with their own goals and often working in isolation from each other. This isn't just inefficient—it's counterproductive. Creative leadership, on the other hand, breaks down these walls. It encourages collaboration across departments, recognizing that great ideas can come from anywhere.

As a creative leader, you bring people together from different disciplines— marketing, technology, design, and beyond. You create a space where everyone has a voice and where diverse perspectives are not just welcomed but celebrated. And the result? A collaborative environment where ideas flow freely and where those ideas can actually be brought to life.

c) Adapting to Change and Driving Innovation

Traditional leaders, in many cases, are risk-averse. They prioritize maintaining the status quo keeping things stable and predictable. While that may be beneficial in certain industries, in marketing, this approach is a huge disadvantage. Marketing is all about change—it's constantly evolving, just like the consumer behaviours we're trying to reach. Creative leaders thrive in this environment. They don't see disruption as a threat. They see it as an opportunity.

These leaders are change-makers, constantly looking for new ways to improve processes, enhance experiences, and push the boundaries of what's possible. They embrace new technology, they experiment with fresh platforms, and they aren't afraid to fail. They know that each mistake is just another step toward greater success.

2. The Importance of Vision and Creativity in Business Leadership

In the past, business leaders focused on the practical stuff: managing operations, ensuring profitability, and hitting short-term goals. And don't get me wrong, those things are still important. But today's marketing leaders need more. They need vision. They need an unwavering belief in creativity's power to drive long-term success.

a) Vision: A Roadmap for Innovation

Here's the thing: creativity alone isn't enough. A truly successful creative leader has a clear vision for where they want the business to go. That vision is the roadmap—it gives direction, purpose, and focus. It helps teams align their efforts toward a common goal. And a leader with a creative mindset doesn't just live in the present—they're always thinking ahead. What's coming next? What new technology is on the horizon? What's the next big trend?

For creative leaders, vision often revolves around innovation. It's not just about growth; it's about shaping the future. It's about connecting with customers in new, exciting ways, telling stories that resonate, and building brands that people genuinely care about.

b) Creativity as a Catalyst for Problem-Solving

Now, creativity isn't just about coming up with new marketing ideas. It's also about solving problems—big, complex problems. Today's leaders face so many challenges, from navigating economic uncertainty to managing organizational change. Creative leaders bring a fresh perspective to these challenges. They don't just rely on conventional solutions—they think outside the box, approaching problems with innovative solutions that others might miss.

Take a crisis, for example. When the usual answers aren't enough, creative leaders step up. They reimagine strategies, find new ways to engage customers and embrace emerging trends that keep the business relevant and thriving.

c) Inspiring Others Through Creativity

A creative vision isn't worth much if you can't inspire others to embrace it. The best creative leaders are those who can communicate their vision clearly, making it compelling and inspiring. They don't just dictate—they motivate. They create an environment where creativity is celebrated and where employees feel a deep sense of ownership and excitement about their work. And when people feel their contributions matter, they give their best.

Inspiring creativity also means creating a safe space for people to share their ideas—without fear of judgment. Creative leaders encourage open dialogue and make it clear that innovation is encouraged—even if it means taking risks or making mistakes. This culture of creativity leads to happier, more engaged teams— and, in turn, better outcomes for the business.

Developing a Creative Mindset

In today's fast-paced, ever-changing business world, creativity is no longer just a nice-to-have; it's a must. We're living in an age where industries are constantly evolving, embracing innovation, and adapting to new technologies at lightning speed. For leaders, this means that fostering a creative mindset within their teams isn't just important—it's absolutely critical. Creativity isn't just about coming up with shiny new ideas; it's about tackling challenges from fresh angles, building environments that nurture innovation and step away from the traditional, often limiting, ways of thinking.

In this section, I'll walk you through how to cultivate creativity in your business, how to overcome those frustrating creative blocks we all face, and how to use curiosity and open-mindedness as powerful tools for leadership. When you understand and embrace these strategies, you'll unlock the full potential of your team and set them on the path to success in an ever-evolving market.

1. How to Cultivate Creativity in Business

We often think of creativity as something reserved for artists or designers, but here's the truth—creativity is essential across the board, from marketing to finance, from management to product development. It's the secret weapon that allows teams to approach problems in bold, new ways and stay one step ahead of the competition.

a) Encourage a Growth-Oriented Environment

The first thing you need to do is foster a growth mindset within your organization. Now, I know that might sound a bit cliché, but hear me out: a growth mindset means believing that creativity and intelligence aren't fixed traits. They can be developed over time through effort, practice, and, most importantly, the willingness to learn from failure. Creating a space where failure isn't feared but seen as part of the journey is key to building a truly creative culture.

You can promote this mindset by offering continuous learning opportunities— whether that's workshops, seminars, or even informal brainstorming sessions. By framing challenges as learning opportunities, you'll inspire your team to tackle tough problems with energy and enthusiasm. When people aren't afraid of failure, they're more likely to take risks and think creatively.

b) Create an Open Space for Ideas

For creativity to thrive, the environment has to support it. Rigid hierarchies and restrictive organizational structures can stifle innovation before it even has a chance to grow. As a leader, your job is to tear down those walls and create a space where ideas can flow freely. Encourage open communication and cross-departmental collaboration. When everyone—from the intern to the CEO—feels that their voice matters, creativity flourishes.

Regular brainstorming sessions are a great way to do this. In these sessions, every idea is valuable, no matter how unconventional it may seem. When people feel heard and empowered, they're more likely to bring their best, most creative selves to the table. This inclusivity builds a sense of ownership and passion, pushing your team to think outside the box.

c) Embrace Diversity and Cross-Disciplinary Collaboration

Diversity is a game-changer when it comes to creativity. When people from different backgrounds, cultures, and disciplines come together, the ideas that emerge are unlike anything you'd get in a more homogenous environment. Each person brings a unique perspective, which leads to more creative and innovative solutions.

As a leader, you should actively encourage cross-disciplinary collaboration. Whether it's having your marketing team work alongside product development or bringing tech experts into the creative process, mixing things up sparks fresh ideas. Diverse teams think differently, and that's where the magic happens.

2. Overcoming Creative Blocks in Marketing Strategy

Let's be real—no matter how talented we are, we all face creative blocks. Whether it's struggling to come up with the next big campaign or finding ourselves stuck in a rut with repetitive strategies, creative blocks are a natural part of the creative process. But here's the good news: overcoming these blocks is a skill that you, as a leader, can master.

a) Embrace Constraints as Creative Fuel

Here's a little secret: creativity doesn't always thrive in an environment of unlimited freedom. In fact, constraints—whether they're in terms of budget, time, or resources—can actually spark the best ideas. Think about it: when you're limited, you have to get creative and find innovative ways to make things work.

Instead of seeing constraints as roadblocks, encourage your team to view them as opportunities. Working within limitations forces your team to dig deeper, challenge the status quo, and come up with ideas that are both original and resourceful. Constraints aren't enemies; they're just a little nudge that helps sharpen creativity.

b) Change Your Environment

Sometimes, the best way to break through a creative block is to simply change your environment. A change of scenery, whether it's stepping outside the office or working in a new space, can refresh your mind and give you new perspectives. Encourage your team to take a break, get outside, and come back with a renewed sense of creativity. You might even consider hosting team brainstorming sessions in unconventional places, like a coffee shop or a park—places that allow for fresh thinking.

It's not just about getting out of the office, though. Inside the workplace, small changes can also make a big difference. Set up spaces where people can relax, reflect, and have informal discussions. Create areas that spark creativity—maybe a cosy lounge or a space dedicated to spontaneous team huddles. Little shifts like these can make a big impact.

c) Encourage Collaboration with External Creators

When you hit a creative block, sometimes the solution is simply to look outside your immediate circle. Working with external creators—whether that's freelancers, artists, or industry experts—can inject fresh energy and perspectives into your projects. External collaboration helps challenge your team's assumptions and provides new, innovative ideas.

Bring in guest speakers, collaborate with consultants or partner with influencers. External creators bring diversity of thought, and that can often be just what your team needs to break free from creative stagnation.

3. The Role of Curiosity and Open-Mindedness in Leadership

Curiosity and open-mindedness might not always be at the forefront of leadership discussions, but trust me, they're two of the most important qualities any creative leader can have. Curiosity helps you stay adaptable, constantly learning, and always ready to embrace new ideas. Open-mindedness keeps you receptive to new ways of thinking, even when they challenge your own beliefs.

a) The Power of Questioning Assumptions

Curiosity drives you to ask tough questions. Instead of just asking, "How can we sell more?" ask, "What problem does our product solve for the customer?" Or, "How can we improve the experience for our customers in ways others haven't thought of?" These kinds of questions push you to uncover hidden opportunities and go deeper than surface-level solutions.

b) Remaining Open to New Ideas

An open mind is just as essential. A creative leader embraces ideas, no matter how radical they might seem. By remaining open-minded, you create a culture where employees feel safe sharing their thoughts without fear of judgment. This willingness to listen sparks new ideas and keeps creativity alive throughout the organization.

c) Encouraging Exploration and Experimentation

Curiosity also means being willing to explore and experiment. Let your team try new things, test out new ideas, and see what sticks. This kind of experimentation leads to discovery. And yes, it means there will be some missteps along the way, but that's how you learn and grow. Encourage calculated risks and help your team see failure as a stepping stone toward success.

Developing a creative mindset isn't a one-time thing—it's a journey. It's about continually fostering curiosity, overcoming creative blocks, and creating an environment where ideas can thrive. As a leader, embracing this mindset will help you inspire your team, drive innovation, and lead your organization to success in today's competitive marketplace.

Building a Diverse and Inclusive Creative Team

Let's talk about something close to the heart of every truly innovative brand: diversity and inclusion. In today's marketing and innovation landscape, these aren't just buzzwords or HR goals—they're absolute necessities. When you bring together individuals from different backgrounds, experiences, and perspectives, you ignite a kind of magic that no algorithm can replicate. Creative brilliance doesn't happen in an echo chamber. It happens when people who see the world differently come together and listen, learn, and create something new—together.

In this section, I want to explore with you why diverse perspectives aren't just nice to have—they're essential for sparking real creativity. We'll also dive into how you can foster a workplace culture where inclusion isn't just policy—it's a way of thinking and leading. And to make this real, I'll walk you through a few powerful case studies where inclusive, diverse creative teams have changed the game. These aren't just stories—they're proof that the future belongs to those who make space for everyone.

1. Why Diverse Perspectives Lead to Better Creativity

Let me be clear: when I say "diversity," I'm not just referring to race or gender. It includes differences in lived experiences, socioeconomic backgrounds, disciplines, generations, languages, belief systems—even how people think and process information. In creativity, that variety isn't just beneficial—it's rocket fuel. Why? Because real innovation happens when you challenge the norm, and that challenge often comes from people who see the world differently.

a) Exposure to Varied Experiences and Ideas

Think about your own life for a moment. How many times has a conversation with someone from a completely different walk of life opened your eyes to a new way of thinking? That's what happens on diverse teams every day. A marketer with a background in sociology, for example, will bring a different lens to audience behaviour than someone from an engineering background. Now imagine putting them in the same room to brainstorm. That's where the sparks fly.

When we draw from various cultures, professions, and life stories, we start connecting dots others don't even see. That's not just creativity—that's creative depth. And it's not theory. Studies consistently show that diverse teams solve problems faster, develop more innovative solutions, and outperform more homogenous groups. Simply put, they get things done better and smarter.

b) Breaking Down Groupthink

Let's be honest. It's easy—and comfortable—to be around people who think like us. But comfort is the enemy of innovation. Groupthink, that dangerous lull of agreement, sneaks in when teams are too similar in thought and background. It limits risk-taking, waters down creativity, and eventually leads to mediocrity.

When you build a team that isn't afraid to disagree—or sees things in ways you never considered—you disrupt that sameness. Yes, it can be messy at times. But that friction? That's where the magic happens. Diversity introduces healthy tension and, with it, the possibility for new, bold, and brilliant ideas.

c) Meeting the Needs of Global Audiences

We live in a world that's beautifully complex and wildly interconnected. What resonates in New York might fall flat in Nairobi— or Tokyo, or Mumbai. To create marketing that truly connects with people, we have to understand them. Their culture. Their humor. Their pain points and aspirations. That kind of insight doesn't come from guesswork; it comes from representation.

When your team includes people who reflect the diversity of your audience, your campaigns become more authentic and your messaging more meaningful. You avoid the clichés the tone-deaf blunders, and instead tell stories that truly resonate. That's not just smart marketing— it's respectful, human marketing. And in today's world, that's what builds lasting loyalty.

2. How to Foster Inclusive Creative Environments

Now, let's be real. Diversity without inclusion is just window dressing. It's not enough to have people from different backgrounds in the room—you need to make sure they feel seen, heard, and empowered to contribute. Inclusion is where diversity comes alive. It's where voices get amplified, not just invited.

a) Create an Open Dialogue and Safe Space

If you want people to share their best ideas, they need to feel safe doing it. That means creating a culture where it's okay to speak up, where no one's laughed at or shut down for thinking differently. And it starts with you—the leader. Are you actively listening? Are you making space for the quiet voices in the room?

Make time for one-on-one check-ins. Celebrate vulnerability. Set the tone that it's okay to not have all the answers. The more you normalize openness and honesty, the more your team will start showing up with courage—and creativity.

b) Implement Policies that Promote Inclusion

Let's move beyond good intentions. Inclusion requires intentional systems and policies. Are your hiring practices equitable? Do you offer mentorship for underrepresented groups? Is unconscious bias training part of your leadership development?

Your policies should say, loud and clear, "You belong here." Accessibility, equal growth opportunities, and clear anti-discrimination structures aren't just good ethics—they're essential to cultivating trust. And when trust exists, creativity flows freely.

c) Encourage Diverse Representation in Leadership

Representation matters—especially at the top. When people see leaders who look like them or who share aspects of their background, it changes how they view their own potential. It tells them, "There's space for you at the table."

As leaders, we have to be intentional about who we elevate. Are we creating leadership pipelines for diverse talent? Are we promoting based on merit *and* equity? Remember, diverse leadership doesn't just reflect your values—it drives smarter, more inclusive decisions for your entire organization.

3. Case Studies of Creative Teams Driving Innovation

Still wondering if diversity really impacts creativity? Let's look at a few real-world examples of companies that made inclusion a priority—and reaped the rewards of innovation, relevance, and brand loyalty.

a) Apple's Diverse Team and Its Impact on Product Design

Apple is known for its sleek design and user-friendly products, but what often goes unnoticed is the diversity behind those innovations. Apple has intentionally built teams that blend artistic vision with technical excellence—from various countries, cultures, and disciplines.

This diversity shows up in their product features, accessibility functions, and global appeal. Their marketing campaigns speak to universal human emotions because they're created by teams who understand those emotions from lived experience. That's not just design thinking—it's human-centered innovation powered by inclusion.

b) Nike's "Dream Crazy" Campaign: Embracing Diversity to Drive Social Change

When Nike launched the "Dream Crazy" campaign with Colin Kaepernick, they took a huge risk. But it was a calculated, values-driven one. The campaign wasn't just about sports—it was about identity, belief, and justice. It resonated because it reflected the diversity and real-life struggles of its audience.

Nike showed us that creativity can be brave—that it can take a stand. And that diversity isn't just about hiring practices; it's about whose stories you choose to tell. Their campaign didn't just trend—it sparked global dialogue and deepened brand loyalty among a new generation of consumers.

c) Google's Diversity Initiatives: Building a Culture of Innovation

Google's "Year in Search" campaigns don't just showcase technology—they showcase humanity. That's intentional. The company has invested heavily in building diverse teams, and it shows in how they tell stories, solve problems, and build products.

From gender-neutral job listings to inclusive onboarding practices, Google understands that innovation starts with the people in the room. Their emphasis on equity and representation has not only made their workforce stronger—it's made their brand more empathetic, relevant, and future-ready.

Building a diverse and inclusive creative team isn't a checkbox—it's a commitment. It's a recognition that the best ideas don't come from comfort zones. They come from courageous conversations, from different perspectives, meeting in a space of mutual respect. And most of all, they come from leaders—like you— who believe in building not just great products or campaigns, but great cultures.

When we choose inclusion, we don't just open the door for others—we open the door for innovation. And in a world that changes by the minute, that kind of creativity isn't just valuable—it's vital.

Throughout this chapter, we've delved into what creative leadership truly means. It's not just about coming up with brilliant ideas—it's about something much deeper. It's about creating an environment where creativity isn't just encouraged but nurtured. A place where every person on your team feels that spark of inspiration, where they feel safe and empowered to contribute their thoughts, their vision, and their unique perspective.

In that space, creativity can thrive—like a garden full of diverse flowers, each one offering something new and exciting to the mix. As a leader, you have the incredible responsibility and the incredible opportunity to shape that space. It starts with developing a creative mindset, one that isn't bound by limitations or the old ways of thinking. It's about breaking free from barriers, overcoming the fears that hold back innovation, and building a team that reflects the world we live in—diverse, inclusive, and full of potential.

This isn't just about making your organization better; it's about shaping the future. The future of your team, your company, and even the industry you're a part of. The choices you make today will ripple out into tomorrow. As the world evolves at an astonishing rate, the need for fresh, bold ideas is more urgent than ever. It's no longer enough to simply keep up with change—you have to drive it. Lead with vision. Lead with passion. And lead with the understanding that creativity is the spark that will light the way forward.

So, encourage curiosity. Create a space where new ideas can be breathed. Embrace the diversity of thought that each person brings. It's not just about pushing boundaries in the work you do; it's about creating a culture where your team pushes boundaries together. When creativity is woven into the very fabric of your organization, you'll see the results—not just in the innovative products and campaigns you create, but in the way your team interacts with one another, in how they collaborate, and in how they rise to every challenge together.

The Creative Corridor Awaits

But here's the thing—this journey doesn't have an end. The creative corridor isn't a destination. It's a path. A never-ending, exhilarating path paved by those who refuse to accept the status quo. Those who are willing to take risks, to step outside the comfort zone, and to lead with vision. You're one of those people. You have it in you to be the catalyst for change, for innovation, for transformation.

As you walk down this path, always remember creativity is not just a tool—it's the very lifeblood of success in our world today. It's the thing that will keep you ahead of the curve and keep you pushing forward when others are stuck. Whether you're breaking through your own creative blocks, building a diverse team, or fostering a culture of inclusion and innovation, your leadership can inspire something bigger than yourself. It can ignite a movement.

So, take this journey with an open heart. Don't just go through the motions— embrace it. Embrace the challenges, the growth, the victories, and the setbacks. Know that the future of your organization, your team, and your industry is waiting for you to step up to lead them into a brighter, more creative tomorrow. The world is changing rapidly, and you have the incredible opportunity to be the one who helps shape it. The opportunity to stand at the forefront of that change, to push the boundaries of what's possible, is yours.

Let creativity be your guide. Let it fuel every decision, every challenge, every breakthrough. The possibilities that lie ahead are endless—yours to shape, yours to discover.

The creative corridor is waiting for you. All you have to do is step into it with open arms and an open mind and let the world see what you're capable of.

Chapter 8
The Rise of the Creative Entrepreneur

Let's take a moment to really think about what it means to be an entrepreneur today.

In the past, when we thought of entrepreneurship, we often pictured a traditional path—starting a business, managing finances, scaling an idea. The focus was always on products, services, and numbers. But that's changing, and the shift is nothing short of exhilarating. The world is witnessing the rise of the *creative entrepreneur*, a new breed of business leader who is blending artistry with innovation and is building businesses that aren't just profitable but also *purposeful*. These entrepreneurs are weaving creativity into the very fabric of their ventures—redefining the way we think about success.

The creative entrepreneur doesn't just create something for the sake of profit; they create something with passion with heart. Whether it's a digital product, an artistic vision, or a cultural movement, they understand that their work can spark conversations, challenge norms, and change lives. They're not bound by traditional structures or industries. They're creating businesses that exist in a space between art, commerce, and social impact.

This chapter is about celebrating that shift—the rise of these new-age entrepreneurs who are redefining what it means to succeed in the modern world. The creative entrepreneur is someone who doesn't just adapt to change—they *create* it. They see opportunities where others see obstacles, and they use their creativity to navigate and thrive in a world that's constantly evolving.

So, what does it mean to be a creative entrepreneur in today's age? What does it take to truly build something meaningful that lasts? How do these individuals make their mark and rise above the noise of a world saturated with ideas?

As we dive into this chapter, we'll explore these questions and more. We'll look at how entrepreneurship is being redefined in this new creative age. We'll discuss the tools, platforms, and mindsets that are empowering creative entrepreneurs to turn their visions into reality. And we'll also take a closer look at how we can nurture the next generation of creative leaders—those who will continue to push boundaries, challenge conventions, and shape the future of entrepreneurship.

The creative economy is here, and it's changing everything. It's shifting the way we think about work, about value, about what it means to build a lasting legacy. The people driving this change are the creative entrepreneurs—the dreamers, the risk-takers, the innovators who are daring to think differently and build businesses that speak to the heart of what it means to be human.

Are you ready to explore how creativity is shaping the future of entrepreneurship? Let's take this journey together and discover what it truly takes to rise as a creative entrepreneur in today's world.

Redefining Entrepreneurship in the Creative Age

I still remember the first time someone looked me in the eye and asked, "So, are you an entrepreneur?"

I paused.

Not because I didn't have an answer but because I wasn't sure if my answer would fit into what the world traditionally expected. I didn't have a tech startup. I hadn't pitched to a panel of investors, nor had I ever stepped foot into a boardroom wearing a suit. I wasn't drawing up balance sheets or crafting exit strategies.

But I had something else.

I had ideas. Raw, messy, stubborn ideas that kept me up at night. I had this relentless desire to build—something personal, something that mattered, something that could move people. And that, as I would come to realise later, was the very spark of entrepreneurship. Not the polished pitch deck. Not the business card. Just that fire.

We're living in a new era now—one where the image of an *"entrepreneur"* has expanded far beyond the old definitions. You don't have to be sitting in Silicon Valley, coding the next big app. You don't have to speak in corporate jargon or wear a name badge that says *"CEO."*

Today's entrepreneurs are found in the corners of coffee shops, at kitchen tables, or sitting cross-legged on apartment floors with a laptop and a dream.

They're storytellers, artists, designers, poets, podcasters, and YouTubers. They're building from emotion, from culture, from creativity.

They're launching fashion brands with a purpose, writing newsletters that spark communities, and crowdfunding passion projects that raise awareness and drive change.

And most of all—they're doing it their way.

Let me tell you something I've learned first-hand:

You don't need permission to start.

You don't need an MBA to launch a brand that speaks to people. You don't need to rent an office or wait for someone else to give you a green light.

What you need is **vision**.

The kind that makes your heart race and your voice shake a little when you talk about it.

You need **courage**—

The kind that helps you keep going even when the likes don't come, the sales don't show up, and the world doesn't quite get it yet.

And you need **resilience**—

Because failure isn't just possible, it's inevitable. But guess what? Failure isn't the end—it's the lesson, the re-route, the step forward.

Creative entrepreneurs don't just think outside the box—they reshape the box. Sometimes, they throw the box out entirely. Because the truth is, they've never really fit into one to begin with.

They blend imagination with action.

They turn their creativity into currency—not just in terms of income, but in terms of impact.

They blur the boundaries between art and commerce, passion and profession, purpose and profit. And when they show up—raw, real, and willing—they change the narrative of what leadership looks like in this generation.

You see, we've been taught for so long that entrepreneurship is about scalability, about systems, about numbers.

But now, it's just as much about **stories**. About **soul**.

About how something makes people **feel**.

Sometimes, entrepreneurship doesn't look like building a team or pitching on stage. Sometimes, it looks like staying up until 2 a.m. tweaking your portfolio. It looks like designing your own logo when you can't afford a graphic designer. It looks like making ten cold calls a day, recording content between shifts, or writing blog posts during your lunch break.

It looks like care. Like heart. Like *hope* in motion.

It's that moment when someone messages you to say, *"Your work helped me,"* and your chest tightens because that's why you started in the first place.

It's the quiet wins, the small beginnings, the voice inside that whispers, *"Keep going,"* even when the world feels impossibly loud with doubt.

If you're someone who's always been a little different—

If your ideas don't seem to fit into traditional moulds, if your path feels uncharted, if you've ever felt like the world wasn't quite built for the way you think—

Then maybe, just maybe, you're already a creative entrepreneur.

You don't have to raise millions to matter.

You don't have to be on a Forbes list to be doing the work.

All you need is something honest to say, something brave to create, and the guts to keep showing up.

So, if no one's told you yet— Yes. You are an entrepreneur.

And the world needs what *only you* can build.

This is your permission. This is your moment. This is your start. Let it be messy. Let it be real. Let it be yours.

Tools, Platforms, and Mindsets for Creative Entrepreneurs

Let's take a moment to acknowledge something we all know deep down: being a creative entrepreneur isn't exactly a walk in the park. I know, I know—you're probably thinking, "No kidding." But hear me out for a second. When we think about creative entrepreneurship, what do we typically picture? We imagine a bright-eyed visionary with endless ideas, churning out product after product, all the while staying motivated and inspired. We see them getting a standing ovation after every launch, basking in the glow of success and admiration. Sounds wonderful, right? If only it were that simple.

The truth? It's a lot messier than that.

At first, it's thrilling, of course. That moment when your idea sparks to life, when you start building something from scratch, it's intoxicating. It feels like you're on top of the world. But then, reality sets in. The uncertainty, the unpredictability, and yes, the fear. You wake up full of energy and inspiration, ready to conquer the day. But by lunchtime, you're second-guessing everything. You wonder if anyone cares about what you're creating. You start questioning your worth, your talents, and even your purpose in this journey. *Am I really cut out for this?* You wonder. Sound familiar?

I want you to know something: this inner turmoil you're feeling, this self-doubt that creeps in, it's not a sign of weakness. It's a sign that you're doing something important. If you're feeling the uncertainty, it's because you're taking risks, pushing boundaries, and creating something that hasn't existed before. And that? That's what it means to be a creative entrepreneur.

And here's the best part: You're living at a time when the world has never been more ripe for creative entrepreneurship. If you had a vision like the one you have today, even just a few decades ago, you would have had to jump through countless hoops, take out massive loans, and possibly give away much of your creative control just to get a small piece of the pie. But not anymore. We are standing at the dawn of the digital age, and it is *your* greatest ally.

Are the tools available today? They're game-changers. Platforms like Shopify, Etsy, Substack, and Patreon have completely transformed the entrepreneurial landscape. These platforms have radically flattened the barriers that once stood between you and the world. No longer do you need a warehouse full of inventory or a massive team to launch a successful business? Your living room can be your studio, your kitchen table, your showroom, your bedroom, your stage. *All* you need is a laptop, an internet connection, and a dream.

The Digital Age: Empowering the Creative Visionary

You might be wondering: why is the digital age so empowering for creative entrepreneurs? Well, think about it for a moment. The internet has transformed the very concept of *access*. You can now reach an audience on the other side of the world from the comfort of your own home. Whether you're a musician, a writer, a designer, or a craftsman, you can now put your work in front of people who care about it—no matter where they are.

But it goes beyond just the ability to connect with a global audience. The digital age has given us the power to bypass traditional gatekeepers. In the past, getting your art or product into the world required jumping through hoops, whether that meant convincing a publisher to pick up your book or begging a buyer at a department store to carry your line. Today, you don't need to wait for someone else's approval. With platforms like Etsy, Shopify, and Substack, you can launch your product or service directly to the market. You are in control of your success— or failure.

Moreover, the cost of entry has dramatically decreased. For instance, a few years ago, opening a brick-and-mortar store required significant capital to secure a location, staff it, and maintain inventory. But now, for the cost of a domain name and a Shopify subscription, you can open an online store and start selling to a global audience within a matter of hours.

This is not just a game-changer—it's a *paradigm shift* in how business is done. The barriers to entry have been removed, which means the playing field has been levelled. In the past, success was often tied to proximity, location, and who you knew. Now, with the internet, all you need is an idea and a drive to make it happen. And it's this very shift that empowers you, as a creative entrepreneur, to take control of your own destiny.

But There's More Than Just Tools—The Mindset is Key

While these platforms and tools are undeniably powerful, there's something even more important that determines your success as a creative entrepreneur: your mindset. Sure, the tools make it easier to get your idea out there. But the right mindset will carry you through the inevitable challenges and moments of doubt.

The most successful creative entrepreneurs I've encountered aren't necessarily the ones with the most resources or the best technology. They're the ones who stay curious and ask themselves, "What if?" every single day. This mindset—one of curiosity and continual learning—is essential. The digital world moves fast, and if you're not willing to experiment, adapt, and learn along the way, you'll find yourself left behind.

Being a creative entrepreneur is about more than just jumping on the latest trend. It's about tapping into your creativity in a way that feels authentic, true to your values, and relevant to the world around you. It's about asking yourself, "What does my audience need right now? How can I solve a problem for them? How can I bring something into the world that will make a meaningful difference?"

This is where your values come into play. One of the most important qualities of a successful creative entrepreneur is being values-driven. You're not just creating a product to make money. You're creating something that matters. And when you align your business with your values, the result is something that doesn't just sell— it *connects*. The best businesses are those that stand for something bigger than just their bottom line.

Take, for example, brands like Patagonia or Ben & Jerry's. They're not just about selling products—they've created movements. They stand for something that resonates with their customers, and in turn, their customers stand by them. This is the power of having a strong, values-driven brand. It's not just about the product— it's about the story you're telling and the impact you're making.

The Power of Community: You're Not Alone

Let's talk about community for a minute. As a creative entrepreneur, you're probably used to working alone. It's natural, especially when you're in the early stages of your business. You have a vision, and you're driven to make it happen. But what I've learned throughout my journey is that the most successful creative entrepreneurs don't do it alone.

They build communities.

Whether it's a group of like-minded individuals online or a physical co-working space, the act of collaborating with others is what propels you forward. Creativity thrives in the community. I'm not saying you have to share every idea or give away all your secrets, but surrounding yourself with other creative people who share your vision can fuel your own growth in ways you can't imagine.

The truth is, as a solo entrepreneur, you'll hit walls. You'll get stuck, unsure of your next step. But when you have a community, whether it's a mentor, a group of fellow entrepreneurs, or an online forum, you have access to a wealth of experience and wisdom. It's these connections that provide fresh perspectives, new ideas, and the emotional support you need to push through the tough times.

Think about it: some of the most successful entrepreneurs in the world—whether in tech, fashion, or entertainment—attribute their success to the communities they've built around them. They didn't just rely on their own talents; they connected with others who brought complementary skills, ideas, and energy to the table. This is where the magic happens. When you collaborate, you open up new possibilities that you may never have considered on your own.

And it's not just about the *big names* in your industry. The power of community can be found in small, niche groups, too. Whether you're a jewellery maker on Etsy or a freelance writer on Substack, there are communities for you. These are spaces where you can share your wins and struggles, get feedback, and even partner on projects. The best part? These communities are often a source of accountability. They push you to keep going when you want to give up and celebrate with you when you achieve milestones.

Embracing Your Unique Voice

One of the biggest mistakes I see many creative entrepreneurs make is doubting their own unique voice. They look at others in their field—successful entrepreneurs who seem to have it all together—and wonder why their own work doesn't measure up. But here's the truth: the world doesn't need another generic product or service. It doesn't need a copycat. What the world needs is *your* voice, your perspective, and your unique point of view. That's your unfair advantage.

You see, there's no one else who sees the world the way you do. No one else has lived your experiences, faced your challenges, or seen the opportunities you've seen. That makes your perspective invaluable. And it's this authenticity that will set you apart from the rest.

So when you're feeling overwhelmed, uncertain, or even jealous of others' success, remember: *there's no competition when you're being yourself.* What the world wants is your *truth*. That's what will connect you with the right people and build a lasting, meaningful business.

Your Creative Journey Awaits

Let me start by saying this: I know the road ahead won't always be easy. There will be moments—more than you can count—when you question yourself, when doubt creeps in, and when everything feels harder than it should. You'll find yourself facing challenges, sometimes ones that feel insurmountable. You'll encounter rejection, and there will be times when the path forward seems unclear.

But here's something I need you to understand, deep down: this journey, the one you're about to embark on as a creative entrepreneur, is worth every moment of struggle. It's worth it because every moment of doubt and every roadblock you hit is part of your evolution. It's part of what will shape you into the kind of entrepreneur who can build not just a business but a legacy—something meaningful, something impactful, something that connects with others in ways you can't even imagine yet.

And let's be clear about one thing: the tools, platforms, and mindsets that are available to you today have never been more empowering. Never before has it been possible to launch your creative idea into the world with such ease. Never before has it been so accessible to build an audience, to connect with people, to share your passion, and to make an impact. The world is more connected than ever, and you, with your creativity and vision, have the unique opportunity to tap into this global landscape.

So, what are you waiting for? Take that first step.

I know it sounds easier said than done. There's always a voice in the back of your mind telling you it's not the right time, that you need more preparation, that you're not ready. But here's the truth: you will never feel completely ready. The perfect moment, the "right time," that mythical window of opportunity—it doesn't exist.

You have to create it. You have to step into it, even when it feels like you're not entirely sure of the way forward.

Because here's the thing: if you wait until you feel ready, you'll never get started. And if you don't start, you'll never know what could have been. The world is waiting for your voice, for your unique perspective, for the magic only you can create. There is someone, somewhere, who needs exactly what you have to offer, even if you don't know them yet. Your work, your creativity, your ideas—they matter.

I'm not asking you to have it all figured out right now. In fact, that's not even the point. The point is to *start*. It's about taking that first step, even if it's a small one because those small steps will eventually lead to something much bigger. They'll lead to breakthroughs, to moments of clarity, to opportunities that you couldn't have seen before. And most importantly, they'll lead to growth—both personal and professional.

The beauty of being a creative entrepreneur today is that you don't have to do it alone. You're not the only one who feels the fear, the uncertainty, the vulnerability of putting yourself out there. There's a vibrant, supportive community of like-minded individuals who are on the same path and who are ready to cheer you on, share advice, and help lift you up when the going gets tough.

Don't underestimate the power of that community. Surround yourself with people who believe in you, who push you, who inspire you to be better. Find mentors who have walked the path before you, who can share their wisdom and help you navigate the challenges ahead. And remember: you don't need to have everything figured out from the start. You just need the courage to begin.

The platforms that are available to you today—social media, online marketplaces, digital tools—are all designed to make your journey easier. You can reach a global audience in ways that were once reserved for big corporations. You can build a brand, tell your story, and create a space where your creativity thrives. The resources are there, just waiting for you to dive in.

So yes, the road will be difficult at times. You'll face setbacks. You'll wonder if you're on the right track. But each of these moments will bring with them a lesson. Every rejection, every failure, every moment of doubt—they'll push you forward, shaping your resilience, deepening your understanding of your craft, and refining your vision. Because the truth is the path to success is rarely linear. There are twists and turns, high points and low points, but they're all part of the process.

I can't promise you that it will always be easy. In fact, I can almost guarantee that there will be moments when you'll want to give up when the weight of it all feels too heavy. But here's something you need to hold onto: *your creativity is a force.* It's what makes you unique. It's what will drive you to keep going when things feel impossible. Your creativity is the foundation on which you'll build everything—your brand, your business, your relationships, your success. When you tap into it, when you let it lead you, there is nothing you cannot achieve.

The world is changing fast. The old systems are being disrupted, and in their place is a new era, one where creativity isn't just a nice-to-have but a necessity. The businesses that thrive, the ones that stand the test of time, are the ones that embrace creativity at their core. The creative entrepreneur is the one who leads the way, not just by building something new but by building something that resonates deeply with people. Something that touches hearts, changes minds, and leaves a lasting impact.

That's where you come in.

You have the opportunity to build something truly meaningful, something that reflects your vision and creativity. You have the power to shape the world in ways that are authentic to who you are and that matter to you and to others. You're not just creating for the sake of creating. You're creating with purpose, with intention, and with the belief that your work can make a difference.

So go ahead and take that first step. Even if it's scary. Even if you don't know where it will lead. The world is waiting for you. Your voice matters, and I believe, without a doubt, that you have what it takes to make an impact.

Now, it's your turn. Take a deep breath, and step forward into your creative journey. The possibilities are endless. The future is yours to create.

Nurturing the Next Wave of Creative Leaders

If there's one thing I know for sure, it's this: for the creative movement to thrive, we need to invest in the next generation of creative entrepreneurs. This isn't just about giving a select few the tools to succeed; it's about building a system that makes creative entrepreneurship accessible to *everyone*. Everyone—no matter their background, no matter where they're from, and no matter what obstacles they face—deserves the chance to make their creative vision a reality.

Now, let's be clear. The idea that creative entrepreneurship is only for the privileged, those with safety nets or a financial cushion to fall back on, is a myth that we must shatter. The truth is the next wave of creative leaders won't come from the typical places we expect. It's not going to be just the art school graduates or the tech entrepreneurs with venture capital in their pockets. It's going to come from the edges, from people who may have never thought it was possible to build a creative business because they didn't have the "right" credentials, the "right" network, or the "right" financial resources.

If we want to truly elevate the creative industries, then it starts with how we support emerging talent. And that starts with creating systems, spaces, and networks that allow everyone to access the tools they need to succeed. We need to meet people where they are—not just where we think they should be.

Mentorship: A Conversation That Changes Everything

One of the most profound things I've learned in my journey is the power of mentorship. There's something incredibly transformative about having someone— someone who's already walked the road you're on— believe in you. It's like a spark that lights a fire. I've had mentors who, with just a few words, shifted my perspective and helped me see a way forward when I thought I had reached a dead end. That one conversation, that single moment of connection, changed everything. It reminded me that I wasn't alone that the struggles I was facing weren't unique to me— and that there was a way out.

This is why mentorship is essential, especially for emerging creative entrepreneurs. Universities, incubators, and creative agencies must not only serve as breeding grounds for new ideas—they must become bridges. These institutions have the resources to connect young creatives with those who've been there before, those who have the battle scars, the stories, and the experience to guide the next generation.

But mentorship isn't just about telling someone what to do. It's about showing them what's possible. It's about opening up a world of opportunities they might not have even known existed. A good mentor doesn't give you all the answers, but they give you the courage to find your own. They share their stories—both the successes and the failures—so you can learn from them. And perhaps most importantly, they *believe in you* when you don't believe in yourself.

And here's the thing: it doesn't just have to be formal mentorship. Sometimes, it's a chat over coffee, a quick exchange of ideas over social media, or a fellow entrepreneur offering advice based on their own journey. In today's connected world, mentorship can happen in so many different ways, and it's more accessible than ever before. You don't have to be in the same room to learn from someone— sometimes, all it takes is one conversation, one click, and the guidance you need could be right there in front of you.

Funding: More Than Just Money

Now, let's talk about one of the most critical aspects of supporting emerging creative leaders—*funding*. But I want to be clear about something. When we talk about funding, we're not just talking about money. Yes, money is important. But it's not just about getting a cheque. It's about getting belief.

So many creative entrepreneurs get stuck in the trap of thinking that they need a large lump sum of money in order to start their business. They believe they need to land that one big investor or secure a huge loan to get started. But that's not the only route. There are alternatives. Crowdfunding has opened up new possibilities for creative businesses. Websites like Kickstarter and GoFundMe have created an entirely new ecosystem where people can support creative ideas they believe in. This is *powerful*. It's not just about raising money—it's about raising belief, enthusiasm, and a community of backers who are invested in your success.

Then, there's the rise of micro-grants and alternative finance models like revenue-based investing. These are changing the game, offering creative entrepreneurs access to funding without the burden of traditional venture capital or loans. Revenue-based investing, for example, allows you to raise funds based on your future earnings. It's a model that aligns more closely with the realities of creative entrepreneurship, where cash flow can fluctuate, and traditional models of financing often don't apply.

But let's be real: while these alternatives are fantastic, we still have a lot of work to do to ensure that all entrepreneurs—especially diverse founders—have equitable access to resources. We need to dismantle the systemic barriers that prevent people from marginalized backgrounds from accessing capital and mentorship. We need to ensure that funding doesn't just go to those who already have privileges or connections. We need to build a system that lifts everyone up, that celebrates diversity, and that levels the playing field for all creative entrepreneurs.

Education: Teaching Creativity and Business in Harmony

Now, let's talk about education. If we want to nurture the next wave of creative leaders, we need to rethink how we teach creativity and entrepreneurship. Traditional education systems often focus on one side of the equation: the "how to create." But that's just one part of the puzzle. The truth is creative entrepreneurs need to know more than just how to create. They need to understand how to pitch, how to price, how to protect their intellectual property, and how to promote their work.

I've seen too many talented creatives struggle because they didn't have the business acumen to support their creative work. They had the vision, the ideas, and the passion, but they didn't know how to take that creativity and turn it into a sustainable business. We need educational systems that honour both sides of the coin—that teach not only how to make art but how to make a living from it.

We need spaces that celebrate the union of creativity and commerce. This is where things get tricky because so many creatives have been taught to see business as the enemy of art. But this is a dangerous myth. In reality, business and creativity are symbiotic. Creativity without business know-how is often short-lived, but business without creativity is often soulless. To truly succeed, creative entrepreneurs need to understand how to balance both.

We need to create educational environments where dreaming big is encouraged, and failure isn't fatal. Where experimentation is embraced and risk-taking is part of the process. We need to teach young creatives that the journey isn't about avoiding failure—it's about learning from it, bouncing back, and trying again.

Celebrating Creative Entrepreneurs: Shaping the Future

And here's the kicker: we need to start celebrating creative entrepreneurs not just as "side hustlers" or hobbyists but as *architects of the future*. It's time we stop thinking of creative entrepreneurs as people with "fun" jobs or niche interests. They are shaping industries. They are shaping communities. They are shaping cultures. They are innovators in the truest sense of the word, and we need to honour that.

When we think about entrepreneurship, we often think of tech giants, finance moguls, or business tycoons. But the truth is, the world of creative entrepreneurship is just as vital, just as transformative. Innovative entrepreneurs are disrupting industries, redefining norms, and inspiring entire movements. They're the ones creating the culture of tomorrow today. And it's time we recognize that.

So, if you're reading this right now and wondering, "Could I be one of them? Could I be a leader in this creative revolution?" Let me tell you—*yes*. You already are. The fact that you're here, that you're curious, that you care about how your creativity can serve something bigger than yourself? That's the spark. That's the beginning.

You are already on the path, whether you realize it or not. And the world needs you to keep going.

The Power of a Single Idea

We are living in a time where a single idea can change a life. Or change the world. We are in an age where creativity is valued more than ever, where innovation is a currency, and where people are hungry for new ways of thinking and being. Your idea might just be the one that shifts the culture, breaks down the barriers, or redefines what's possible.

So, if you're sitting there wondering if your idea is enough, let me answer that for you: *yes*. Your idea is enough. It's more than enough. It's the beginning of something amazing.

The world is waiting for your voice. Waiting for your perspective. And I, for one, can't wait to see what you create.

Chapter 9

The Intersection of Culture and Creativity

In today's world, borders are becoming more fluid, and ideas are moving faster than ever before. In this interconnected, globalized landscape, culture is no longer just an accessory to creative work—it's the very core of it. It's not just the backdrop to everything we create; it's the driving force behind it. You might not always see it at first glance, but culture shapes everything. It influences how we create, how we respond to ideas, and how we engage with the brands and messages that surround us.

Take a moment and think about it. All those creative pieces that have left an impression on you—whether it's the latest ad campaign, a catchy song that you can't get out of your head, or that bold fashion statement, you can't stop admiring— each of these was not only influenced by culture but was born out of it. The creator's cultural environment, their background, the values they grew up with, the society they're a part of— all of it plays a huge role in the way they approach their craft. And it's not just the creators themselves; it's the audience, too. Culture influences how we perceive, interpret, and connect with what's presented to us. It's what makes an ad feel authentic, or an artist's work resonate deeply with us.

Culture is a bridge. It connects us, even when we seem far apart. It gives creative ideas meaning, depth, and relevance. It's the lens through which we understand not only what is being communicated but *why* it matters to us, to our communities, and to the world at large. Whether you're creating or consuming, culture is the thread that binds us together, influencing everything we experience. So, the next time you come across a piece of creativity that moves you, remember: it's not just the concept, the visuals, or the execution that makes it special. It's the culture that flows through it, shaping every element and every emotion.

Let's take a moment to think about that.

Culture is more than just art or tradition. It's the lived experience of a people, their values, their struggles, their joys. It's in the food they eat, the songs they sing, the words they use. Culture is the lens through which we see the world. And that lens colours not just our personal lives but our professional endeavours, especially in creative industries like marketing, advertising, design, and content creation.

If you're working in these fields—or looking to break into them—understanding the deep, intricate relationship between culture and creativity is essential. In fact, it's the key to standing out in a crowded, noisy world. Because when you get the culture right, you don't just create something that resonates—you create something that connects, that speaks directly to people's hearts, that makes them *feel*

something.

But what does it mean to truly understand the intersection between culture and creativity? Well, it's not just about being aware of cultural nuances or knowing which trends are popping up in different regions of the world. It's about recognizing that culture is the foundation upon which all creativity is built. It's about realizing that every piece of creative work is a mirror reflecting the time, place, and people that produced it.

And in the context of today's globalized marketplace, that's more important than ever. As creators and marketers, we're not just competing with others in our own neighbourhoods anymore. We're competing with the entire world. Your message, your brand, and your product can now be seen by someone in Tokyo, New York, Nairobi, or Mumbai—all in a matter of seconds. And if you want to capture their attention, you have to understand their culture. You need to speak their language— not just literally but figuratively, emotionally, and contextually.

That's what we're going to explore in this chapter. We'll look at how culture shapes creative work, how global trends interact with local identities, and how we, as creatives and marketers, can build teams and campaigns that thrive across cultural boundaries. We'll unpack how to tap into the power of culture without exploiting it and how to ensure your creative work is both authentic and inclusive.

It's a big task and one that requires deep empathy, continuous learning, and a willingness to listen. But the rewards? Oh, they're worth it.

So, let's dive into the heart of it.

Understanding the Role of Culture in Creative Work

Culture—it's not just something we study in textbooks or discuss in sociology classes. It's not just a distant concept or a topic for intellectual debates. No, culture is something we live with every day. It's in the music we play, the food we eat, the clothes we wear, and the conversations we have. It's woven into the fabric of our lives, whether we realize it or not. And, perhaps most importantly, culture shapes the way we think and, yes, the way we create.

When I talk about "culture" in this chapter, I'm not referring to some abstract idea or the kind of culture we might observe in an anthropological study. I'm talking about the shared beliefs, values, and practices that define a particular group of people—the very things that shape how they see the world, interact with others, and even respond to the creative work we put out into the world. Think about it: how you see a brand's message, how you interpret an advertisement, or how you connect with a piece of art is influenced by the culture you've grown up in, the values you hold dear and the beliefs that have been passed down through generations.

When we're in the business of creative work, especially in marketing, this cultural foundation becomes even more important. Culture has a massive influence on the way people receive creative work. What works in one country or community might fall flat in another—because, as we know, culture doesn't follow a one-size-fits-all model. Cultural norms, traditions, and values vary widely across regions, and understanding these distinctions is essential when you're crafting campaigns for a global audience. This, my friends, is where the true art of marketing lies. It's not just about selling a product—it's about speaking to people as individuals whose experiences and worldviews are shaped by their culture. It's about tapping into their values, their stories, and their very essence.

Let's pause and think about this for a moment.

Take a global brand like **Coca-Cola**. Its success isn't just a product of great taste and clever marketing. While the product itself remains the same across the globe, Coca-Cola's messaging adapts to fit the cultural context of each market. In one region, the focus might be on family togetherness and community, while in another, it may centre around individuality, adventure, or friendship. Why is that? It's because the Coca-Cola brand understands that people are looking for more than just a refreshing beverage—they're seeking something that resonates with their personal stories. And those stories? They're built on culture—on the environment they grew up in, the values they hold dear, and the traditions that influence their every day.

But it's not just about fitting into a market. It's about understanding how culture can shape your message in ways you might not initially realize. And if you're not careful? You risk missing the mark entirely.

Cultural Sensitivity and Relevance in Campaigns

Cultural sensitivity—now that's a term we hear a lot, but what does it really mean in practice? It's more than just ensuring that your message doesn't offend. Cultural sensitivity goes beyond just avoiding missteps; it's about genuinely *understanding* the nuances of the culture you're working with and using that understanding to inform your creative choices. This is where things get tricky. Because the line between making something relatable and making something tone-deaf is incredibly thin.

Think about the 2018 **"Like a Girl"** campaign by Always. It's a beautiful example of cultural relevance done right. The campaign didn't just tap into the global conversation about gender equality—it dug deeper, addressing the cultural norms and societal expectations that shape how young girls around the world experience self-esteem and confidence. The team behind the campaign didn't just create a generic message about gender empowerment; they understood the cultural touchpoints that would make the message hit home. They knew that for the campaign to resonate, it needed to speak to the specific challenges that young girls face in various parts of the world. It wasn't about making a one-size-fits-all campaign—it was about speaking to diverse audiences in ways that felt true and real to their lived experiences.

When you get this kind of cultural nuance right, you create work that's not just heard but *felt* deeply. It's a campaign that transcends borders and resonates with people on a human level because it acknowledges their culture, their struggles, and their joys. And that's the kind of marketing that sticks with people. The kind that becomes a part of the conversation for years to come.

But here's the catch: failing to consider these cultural elements can have disastrous results. When brands ignore the cultural context of the audience they're speaking to, they risk being seen as tone-deaf, irrelevant, or worse—exploitative. There's a fine line between engaging with culture and appropriating it. Always make sure that when you're using cultural references or tapping into cultural movements, you do so with respect and authenticity.

Cultural Relevance in Digital Marketing

Now, let's talk about the digital landscape—because in today's world, it's where so much of the magic (and the missteps) happen. The rise of social media, blogs, and digital content means that brands can communicate directly with audiences from all corners of the globe. But this speed also means that cultural mistakes can be amplified at a mind-blowing pace. One wrong post, one poorly thought-out video, or a tone-deaf tweet can quickly spiral into a viral disaster.

I'm sure you've seen it happen—brands making headlines for all the wrong reasons because they didn't take cultural nuances into account. It's not just about translating a message into a different language; it's about truly *understanding* the context in which that message is being delivered. The language, the imagery, the humour—it all matters. It all has to align with the cultural sensitivities of your audience.

For example, let's say you're creating an ad for a global audience that uses humour to convey a message. What's funny to someone in the U.S. might not land in Japan. Humour is highly contextual—it's deeply rooted in culture. And so is everything else: what's considered respectful, what's seen as empowering, or even what's seen as offensive can vary drastically depending on where your audience is located.

This is where the beauty of digital marketing comes in. The brands that succeed online are the ones that genuinely understand the cultural fabric of the places they're targeting. They get that it's not just about pushing out a message—it's about building a relationship with your audience. And that relationship is built on trust, empathy, and a shared understanding of what matters to them.

So, how do you build that understanding? How do you ensure your digital marketing isn't just globally visible but culturally relevant? It starts with research—real, deep research. But it also involves listening. Listening to your audience, watching what they share, how they engage, and understanding the conversations they're having. It's about showing up in a way that feels authentic to the people you're trying to reach.

The Power of Culture in Creative Work

Culture isn't just an abstract concept that we pull out of our mental toolbox when we need it. It's the heartbeat of everything we create. It's what breathes life into your ideas, your messages, and your work. Without culture, creativity would have no grounding and no context. It would be like trying to create something beautiful in a vacuum—empty and without meaning. Culture is what makes your message matter. It's what turns a simple ad, a catchy tune, or a striking visual into something that resonates, something that sticks with people long after they've experienced it.

As creators and marketers, our job isn't just to craft messages or create products that sell. It's to tap into the power of culture in a way that elevates, respects, and connects. This is where the true magic happens. When we begin to understand that culture isn't just something to exploit for our own gain—it's something to respect, nurture, and honour—that's when we start to create work that transcends mere transactions and begins to build relationships.

Think about it. Every time you engage with a piece of creative work, whether it's an ad on the street, a brand's Instagram post, or even a viral video, what grabs you isn't just the product or the concept—it's the underlying cultural context. The way it speaks to you, the way it reflects or challenges your values, your identity, and your experiences. That's what makes you pause. That's what makes you connect.

But here's the thing: you can't tap into the power of culture if you don't understand it. If we want to build something that truly resonates with the people we serve, we need to understand them at a deeper level. We need to know their culture—their values, their norms, the little things that make them *them*. It's only when we immerse ourselves in that understanding that we can create work that doesn't just sell a product— it speaks to people's hearts. And that, in the end, is what great creative work is all about. It's not about pushing a product. It's about creating something that feels personal, that feels meaningful.

So, how do we tap into this power of culture? It starts with empathy. It starts with listening. Too often, we assume we know what people want or need, but we don't take the time to truly understand their experiences, their struggles, and their triumphs. When we listen—really listen—we start to hear the stories behind the messages. We begin to understand the unspoken language of culture that drives people's choices and actions. And when we understand that, when we see the world through their eyes, the creative possibilities are endless.

We have to understand that people aren't just consumers. They are living, breathing individuals with rich histories and complex identities. They are shaped by the cultures they come from, by the communities they belong to, and by the experiences that have moulded them. When we recognize this, we stop seeing them as faceless audiences and start seeing them as human beings—people with feelings, desires, and dreams. And then, we can speak to them not just as marketers, but as humans connecting with other humans.

Creating meaningful work also requires us to be willing to challenge ourselves. Sometimes, we need to step out of our own comfort zones and expand our understanding of cultures beyond our own. It's easy to get caught up in our own perspective and forget that the world is a vast, diverse place. But if we truly want to create work that resonates, we must be open to exploring new perspectives, understanding new cultures, and embracing the beauty of diversity. The world is full of stories that haven't been told yet, and the opportunity to create something fresh, something impactful, is only possible when we allow ourselves to be inspired by voices and experiences that may be different from our own.

And let's not forget the role of authenticity in this process. In a world where so many brands are vying for attention, authenticity is the thing that cuts through the noise. People can sense when something is real and when something is just a marketing gimmick. They can tell when a brand genuinely understands and respects its culture and when it's simply trying to capitalize on it for the sake of selling something. Authenticity isn't just a buzzword—it's the foundation of every successful piece of creative work. When your work is authentic, it speaks directly to people's hearts. It doesn't just sell them something—it makes them feel something. And that's the difference between a campaign that fades into obscurity and one that becomes a part of people's lives.

Creating work that respects and elevates culture also means being responsible with the power we hold as creators. With great power comes great responsibility, and when you have the ability to influence people's perceptions, behaviours, and even emotions, you need to use that influence wisely. You need to be conscious of the impact your work can have. This isn't just about crafting something beautiful or clever—it's about creating something that has a positive, lasting effect. It's about fostering a sense of connection, understanding, and respect.

But this is not always easy. The reality is that culture is complex, and tapping into it requires a delicate balance. There's no one-size-fits-all approach to cultural creativity. What works in one context may not work in another, and what's seen as respectful in one culture may be offensive in another. This is where research, insight, and sensitivity come in. You have to be willing to put in the work, to dig deeper, and to understand the nuances of the cultures you're engaging with. This is what separates good creative work from truly great work. It's about being aware of the power you wield and using it with care and respect.

So, how do we ensure that our work resonates? By building bridges instead of walls. By creating something that not only speaks to people's needs but also speaks to their hearts. By creating work that is so much more than just a product—it's a message, a story, a reflection of who they are. When you do that, when you tap into the true power of culture, your work becomes timeless. It becomes something that lasts, something that is remembered.

In the end, this is what great creative work is all about. It's not about selling a product or pushing an agenda. It's about creating something that connects, something that makes people feel seen, heard, and understood. It's about creating work that doesn't just speak to the mind but to the heart. When we create with culture in mind—when we understand the stories, the values, and the people behind the ideas—then we create work that truly matters.

And that, my friends, is the power of culture in creative work. It's what makes your message not just heard but felt. It's what makes your work not just seen but remembered. It's the secret ingredient that transforms good creative into great creative. The next time you sit down to create something, ask yourself: How does this reflect the culture of the people I'm speaking to? How does this tap into the heart of who they are? If you can answer that question, you're on the path to creating something truly powerful.

Global Trends and Local Influences

The world, as we know it, is more connected than ever before. With the internet, social media, and global travel, ideas, trends, and cultural influences are exchanged across borders faster than ever. But while the world is more interconnected, it's also more complex. What starts as a trend in one part of the world can quickly ripple across the globe, but here's the catch: as it travels, that trend doesn't always remain the same. It transforms, adapts, and takes on new meanings depending on where it lands. So, while a trend may begin in one place, it may take on entirely different forms and expressions in another, all shaped by local culture, values, and preferences.

Let's pause for a moment and think about this—because this isn't just about trends; it's about how culture influences everything we create and how we connect with people. **Global trends** are fascinating because they show us the power of shared ideas and the way one moment can spark something bigger than anyone could imagined. But just as a spark can ignite a flame, culture can also change the direction of that flame, shaping it into something entirely unique.

For example, look at **streetwear fashion**—one of the most compelling trends to come out of the urban streets of New York and Los Angeles in the 1980s. Streetwear was born out of the rebellious spirit of skate culture and hip-hop, a way for people to express themselves without adhering to traditional fashion rules. But what's incredible about streetwear is that while it started in one place, it has morphed into a global phenomenon. Fast forward to today, and it's not just a trend in cities like New York or Los Angeles—it's a worldwide movement.

But here's the twist: the way streetwear is expressed has evolved differently depending on where it's embraced. In Japan, for instance, streetwear has evolved into something hyper-stylized, almost high-fashion, blending Western street style with meticulous Japanese attention to detail and design. It's not just about comfort or rebellion anymore; it's become a form of art, an expression of identity that sits at the intersection of fashion and culture. Meanwhile, in other parts of the world, streetwear remains true to its roots—casual, rebellious, and a bold statement of individuality.

Think about the brands that have ridden this global wave, like **Supreme, Off-White,** and **A Bathing Ape**. These brands didn't just settle for a global strategy that was the same everywhere they went. No, they understood the power of local culture. They recognized that in order to truly connect with different regions, they had to understand the

147

unique tastes, symbols, and values of each market. In some places, they release limited-edition collections that speak directly to the local culture. In Japan, for instance, Supreme has launched collaborations with local artists and even tapped into traditional Japanese art forms. They're not just selling clothes—they're selling a cultural experience that aligns with the local context. And this, my friends, is the beauty of global trends—they don't just stay fixed in one place; they evolve, they adapt, and they reflect the richness of diverse cultures.

Bridging Global Trends with Local Culture

Now, as marketers and creative entrepreneurs, we often find ourselves in this fascinating space where global trends collide with local culture. It's like being at the crossroads of two powerful forces. And while it might seem tempting to implement a "one-size-fits-all" approach to your campaigns—because that's often what feels easier, right?—the most successful brands understand the art of *local adaptation*.

Think about **McDonald's**, a global brand with millions of locations in almost every corner of the world. You might think that the same menu would work everywhere, right? After all, a Big Mac is a Big Mac. But McDonald's has something that sets them apart—they know how to *adapt*. Whether it's the **McAloo Tikki** in India, the **Teriyaki McBurger** in Japan, or the **Cheddar Bacon Onion** burger in the U.S., McDonald's doesn't just offer the same thing everywhere—it offers something that reflects the tastes and culinary traditions of each culture it serves. These menu items are not just food—they are a reflection of the local values and culture of each market. The people in each country don't just see McDonald's as a fast-food chain; they see it as a place that respects their traditions understands their preferences, and gives them a taste of something that feels both familiar and new.

And that's what it's all about, isn't it? The magic happens when you can take a global idea, a trend, or a concept and adapt it in a way that resonates with local sensibilities. It's about creating something that feels both relevant *and* authentic. It's about blending the global with the local, the universal with the specific. When you do this right, you're not just creating a product or a service—you're creating an experience that connects with people on a deeper level. And that, my friends, is what the most successful brands do: they understand the power of blending the global and the local.

Challenges of Cultural Adaptation

But here's the thing: adapting to local cultures isn't always as simple as it sounds. It's not a magic formula. It takes time, effort, and, sometimes, a lot of trial and error. After all, there's no blueprint for this kind of work. A campaign that works wonders in one country might need major adjustments before it can work in another. It's a constant process of learning, experimenting, and, most importantly, listening. When you're trying to adapt to a new culture, you have to listen to the people who live it every day. You have to immerse yourself in their way of life, their values, their language, and their history.

But even with the best intentions, things can go wrong. Sometimes, a well-meaning campaign can land flat because it doesn't fully understand the local context, or worse, it inadvertently offends. And trust me, cultural missteps can be costly—not just financially, but in terms of reputation. The last thing you want is for your brand to be seen as tone-deaf or out of touch with the people you're trying to reach.

I'm sure you've heard stories of brands that made huge blunders while trying to adapt to a new culture. Maybe it's a product name that doesn't translate well or an ad that offends the sensibilities of the target market. These mistakes are more than just embarrassing—they can have long-lasting effects on a brand's image. But here's the thing: this isn't a reason to shy away from cultural adaptation. It's a reason to be even more mindful, more careful, and more respectful of the cultures you're trying to connect with.

The key to overcoming these challenges is to always approach cultural adaptation with sensitivity, humility, and a willingness to learn. Every market is different, and every culture is rich with its own complexities. You might stumble, you might make mistakes, but as long as you're listening, learning, and adapting along the way, you're on the right path.

The Beauty of Cultural Adaptation

So, what can we take away from this? **Global trends** have the power to unite us to create shared experiences across borders. But it's the **local cultures** that breathe life into those trends. It's local culture that shapes how we engage with and respond to trends, how we take something global and make it our own. As marketers, creative entrepreneurs, and storytellers, we have a unique opportunity—and responsibility—to understand and respect those cultures and to create work that feels relevant, authentic, and truly reflective of the world we live in.

In the end, it's not about fitting a global trend into a box. It's about embracing the beauty of local cultures and using them to shape something new, something that speaks to people in a way that feels deeply personal and meaningful. And when you get that right? You create work that isn't just successful—it's timeless.

Building Cross-Cultural Creative Teams

As we've delved into the profound connection between culture and creativity, one truth stands out more clearly than ever: creativity is not a solitary, individual endeavour. It's a dynamic, ever-evolving force shaped and fueled by the diverse cultural perspectives that surround us. When we talk about creativity, we're talking about the ways people think, feel, and express themselves—and culture, at its core, is what shapes those very thoughts and emotions.

So, if creativity is shaped by culture, then it stands to reason that the most innovative, forward-thinking, and truly impactful creative teams will be those that are themselves diverse in cultural perspectives. But here's the kicker: in today's globalized world, building a cross-cultural creative team isn't just a smart strategy—it's absolutely essential. The future of creativity depends on our ability to understand, embrace, and celebrate the cultural influences that shape us all.

The Advantages of Cross-Cultural Teams

Let me ask you this: have you ever worked on a team where everyone was from the same background, the same culture, and the same way of thinking? It may have felt easy, right? You all saw the same thing, thought the same way, and approached problems in the same manner. But did it lead to truly innovative or groundbreaking work? Or did it feel more like a lot of ideas bouncing around in a circle with no real spark?

Now, imagine if that same team was made up of people from different cultural backgrounds. Suddenly, every idea is seen through a different lens. A creative brief that might seem straightforward to one person could be perceived entirely differently by someone with a unique cultural perspective. This is where the magic happens. The diversity of thought that comes from working with people who think, speak, and interpret the world differently leads to more dynamic solutions. The result? More creative campaigns, more innovative ideas, and work that feels fresh, authentic, and deeply engaging.

Take global advertising agencies, for example. Many of the most successful agencies put a significant emphasis on diversity in their teams because they know it brings something invaluable to the table—multiple perspectives that, together, create something bigger and more impactful than any one person could have imagined. When people from different backgrounds collaborate, they don't just agree with each other—they challenge each other, ask tough questions, and push each other to think beyond the ordinary.

And that's exactly what we need in creative work—*challenge*. The world we live in is complex, nuanced, and constantly evolving, and the most successful creative teams understand that. They know that by bringing together people with different life experiences, they can craft work that speaks to a wide range of audiences and feels deeply personal to each of them. It's no longer about creating for just one group of people; it's about creating work that resonates across boundaries. And that's the power of cross-cultural collaboration. It leads to work that is more inclusive, empathetic, and truly reflective of the world's diverse audiences.

The Challenge of Building Cross-Cultural Teams

But as exciting and rewarding as it is to work in a cross-cultural team, it's not always easy. It's not just about hiring people from different backgrounds and assuming everything will fall into place. Building a team where cultural diversity thrives requires intentionality, effort, and, most of all, an openness to learning and adapting.

You see, people from different cultures often have different communication styles, work habits, and expectations. In some cultures, people appreciate direct, straightforward feedback—no sugar-coating, no beating around the bush. In other cultures, indirect communication is the norm, and confrontation is avoided. In some regions, decisions are made top-down, with clear hierarchies and authority structures; in others, collaboration and egalitarian decision-making are valued more.

These cultural differences are not bad; they're just different. But if you're not aware of them, they can cause friction within the team. What one person might perceive as a simple exchange of ideas could feel uncomfortable or disrespectful to someone from a different cultural background. And that's where challenges arise. If these differences aren't managed carefully, they can lead to misunderstandings, hurt feelings, and even resentment.

So, what can you do to avoid these pitfalls? The key is creating an environment where respect, openness, and understanding are prioritized. A team that truly values cultural diversity is one where every member feels safe and heard, where their unique perspectives are welcomed, and where differences are celebrated rather than seen as obstacles.

How to Foster a Creative, Inclusive Environment

As a leader or a team member, your role is to help foster an environment where everyone's voice is valued, regardless of their background. This isn't about tokenism—it's about creating a truly inclusive space where everyone feels empowered to contribute their ideas and share their experiences.

One of the most powerful ways to do this is by encouraging cultural competency training. These sessions give team members the opportunity to learn about the cultural backgrounds of their colleagues and gain a deeper understanding of why people think and act the way they do. This kind of training helps break down misunderstandings and bridges gaps in communication. It also shows your team that cultural differences aren't something to be afraid of—they're something to embrace, something to learn from.

But it doesn't stop there. Inclusivity starts with leadership. As a leader, you must model inclusive behaviour. That means actively seeking out diverse perspectives, encouraging cross-cultural exchanges, and creating spaces where all voices can be heard. When team members see that their ideas are valued—when they feel truly respected—they're more likely to share their best, most creative work. And that's when the magic happens.

Fostering a culture of inclusion is not something that can be done overnight. It takes time, patience, and consistent effort. But when it's done right, the results speak for themselves. You'll find that your team is more innovative, more cohesive, and more excited to work together because they know their differences are not just accepted—they're celebrated.

Culture as the Foundation of Creativity

Ultimately, creativity doesn't exist in a vacuum. It's shaped by the world around us, by the people we interact with, and by the cultures we come from. As we continue to navigate the challenges and opportunities of the 21st century, it's becoming increasingly clear that understanding culture is not just a "nice-to-have" for creative professionals—it's a **must-have**.

The most successful campaigns, the most innovative products, and the most impactful creative works will always be those that recognize and harness the power of culture. The future of creativity will be defined by those who can navigate this intersection of culture and creativity with **empathy, respect**, and an openness to learning from the world around them.

So, as you continue on your creative journey, remember this: culture isn't just something that influences your work—it **is** your work. It's the foundation on which everything creative is built. And when you embrace culture—not just your own, but the cultures of those around you—you'll be better equipped to create work that resonates deeply, connects authentically, and drives lasting change.

When it comes to building teams, developing campaigns, and innovating in your field, always remember that the true power of creativity lies in its ability to bridge cultures, bring people together, and create work that reflects the richness and diversity of the world we live in.

Chapter 10
The Future of the Creative Corridor

We are standing on the brink of a new era. The world around us is changing faster than we could have imagined, and with it, the way we create, communicate, and connect is evolving at an extraordinary pace. The walls that once separated industries, cultures, and ideas are no longer as rigid as they used to be. They are dissolving, melting away, and giving birth to new corridors of creativity that span the globe. These corridors, these open paths, are not just physical spaces or markets; they are the very essence of innovation, collaboration, and a future that is being shaped by the ideas we are daring to bring to life today.

Think about it for a moment. The traditional boundaries that once defined industries, such as marketing, entertainment, technology, and design, are now fluid. What does this mean for us? It means that we have more room to explore, to experiment, to connect, and to build. The creative corridor is no longer confined to a specific place or time. It is everywhere, constantly evolving, adapting, and transforming. And with that, the future of creativity is not just about what is happening right now—it's about the journey we are about to embark upon.

As you read these words, I want you to take a moment to think about the trajectory of your own creative journey. What role do you want to play in this rapidly changing landscape? How do you see yourself contributing to the creative economy that is not only reshaping industries but also redefining the way we live and work? The possibilities are endless, and this chapter is designed to help you navigate the future, giving you the tools and insight to become a leader in this exciting, ever-changing world.

The creative landscape has always been dynamic, but now, more than ever, it is alive with the pulse of possibility. The corridors we are talking about are not just bridges between cultures—they are the pathways between industries, between different ways of thinking, and between different ways of creating. They are spaces where the best ideas from all corners of the globe meet, collide, and ultimately give birth to something new. They are the intersections of innovation, where diversity and creativity fuel the fire of progress.

But how do we step into these corridors with purpose? How do we not just become part of the movement but lead it? This chapter is dedicated to answering these questions—because the future is not just for those who wait for change to happen; it's for those who take the reins, who guide the way, and who lead with vision and courage.

In the following sections, we'll take a closer look at the creative corridors that are currently shaping the world. We'll explore the industries, cultures, and forces driving the change, and how you can position yourself as a leader in this creative economy. You will see how marketing leadership is evolving and how you can be at the forefront of this transformation. Together, we will discuss how to shape not just your future but the future of creativity itself.

So, let's dive in. Let's begin this journey through the corridors of the future and discover how you can become a part of this exciting new world. The creative corridor is waiting, and the path ahead is yours to walk.

The Next Wave of Global Marketing

Let's take a deep breath together because we're standing on the edge of something big. This isn't just another phase in the evolution of marketing—it's a complete transformation, one that will shape the future in ways we're just starting to grasp. If you've been in this field for any length of time, you know that the global marketing landscape is constantly changing. Sometimes, it shifts subtly, like a breeze you hardly notice. Other times, it's like an earthquake—sudden, jarring, and impossible to ignore.

And as these changes unfold, they're reshaping not only how brands communicate with consumers but also how we, as marketers, creators, and strategists, show up in the world. The marketing rules of yesterday are being thrown out the window, and we're seeing the rise of new imperatives—things like sustainability, artificial intelligence, and the still-unfolding promise of the metaverse. These aren't just passing trends—they're signposts pointing toward the future of marketing. And you and I? We're here, right in the middle of it, ready to explore, understand, and navigate this new terrain together.

In this section, we're going to dive into three major forces that are driving the next era of global marketing. First up, we'll look at **sustainability**—a movement that's not just a "nice-to-have" but a fundamental shift in how brands must engage with their audiences. Consumers are more conscious than ever before about where their products come from, how they're made, and what impact they have on the world. As marketers, we're no longer just selling a product or service—we're selling a vision for a more sustainable future, and that's something consumers are deeply passionate about.

Next, we'll talk about the **transformative power of artificial intelligence** in creative work. AI is no longer some far-off dream—it's a tool that's here and now, revolutionizing how we think about creativity. From content generation to customer insights, AI is changing everything. But it's not replacing creativity—it's enhancing it, opening up new possibilities and efficiencies we could only dream of a few years ago. It's about using technology to push the boundaries of what's possible without losing the human touch that makes marketing so powerful.

Finally, we'll explore the **immersive frontier of marketing in the metaverse**. Yes, you heard that right—the metaverse. It's not just some abstract concept anymore; it's becoming a reality that's poised to completely reshape the digital landscape. Imagine a space where brands can interact with consumers in ways that are more engaging, more personal, and more immersive than ever before. The metaverse is the next frontier in marketing, and it's where the future of consumer-brand interaction is being redefined.

These three forces—sustainability, AI, and the metaverse—are not just trends to watch. They are signals of what's next, markers of the future we're all building together. And as we move forward, we'll need to be more adaptable, more creative, and more forward-thinking than ever before. The marketing world is evolving at breakneck speed, and the opportunities are endless. But only if we're ready to embrace change, take risks, and lead with purpose. Together, let's step boldly into this new era. The future is waiting for us.

1. The Importance of Sustainability in Marketing

Let's start with something that matters deeply to all of us: the health of our planet and the responsibility we bear as professionals—and as human beings. Sustainability is no longer a niche buzzword whispered in boardrooms. It's a roar coming from consumers, communities, and the conscience of modern brands.

a) Rising Consumer Expectations for Sustainable Practices

People—real people, not just "target audiences"—are looking harder at the choices behind their purchases. They want to know: *Where was this made? Was it done ethically? What impact will it leave behind?* More than ever, especially among Millennials and Gen Z, there's a genuine desire to buy from brands that reflect personal values and a commitment to the greater good.

You might be surprised (or maybe not) to hear that a growing number of consumers are actually willing to pay more—sometimes significantly more—for products that are responsibly sourced, eco-friendly, or aligned with social causes. They're not just spending money; they're casting votes for the kind of world they want to live in.

And here's the thing: sustainability isn't just about recyclable packaging or carbon offsets. It's about transparency. It's about treating workers fairly, sourcing ethically, and contributing to real social impact. Consumers can sense authenticity— and they can sniff out greenwashing in a heartbeat. Miss the mark, and you lose more than a sale; you lose trust.

b) Integrating Sustainability into Brand Identity

To meet this shift, brands must go beyond surface-level gestures.

Sustainability needs to be stitched into the very fabric of your identity. That's more than a marketing campaign—it's a mindset. It's leadership. It means auditing your supply chain, choosing suppliers who share your values, and reducing your footprint wherever you can.

Look at Patagonia. Remember their bold "Don't Buy This Jacket" ad? It wasn't just a clever stunt—it was a values-first statement that inspired consumers to buy less and think more. Or take Tesla: it didn't just sell electric cars; it sold a mission to redefine mobility through innovation and responsibility. These aren't exceptions. They're blueprints.

When sustainability becomes part of a brand's DNA, it becomes a story worth sharing. One that's felt, not just told.

c) *Sustainability as a Competitive Advantage*

Here's a secret most marketers don't talk about enough: doing good is good business. Brands that lead with sustainability don't just win loyalty—they win longevity. Why? Because purpose-driven businesses create deeper emotional connections. They make people feel seen, valued, and aligned.

There's also a smart operational side to this. Switching to renewable energy, reducing waste, and improving supply chain efficiency—these aren't just noble efforts; they're cost-saving moves that pay off in the long run. Imagine that: a win for the planet and a win for the bottom line.

Brands that act now—and act meaningfully—will be the ones that consumers remember, support, and advocate for in the years to come.

2. How Artificial Intelligence is Shaping the Future of Creativity

Now, let's talk about the technology that's changing everything: artificial intelligence. It's no longer a distant dream or a science fiction trope. It's here, right now, and it's transforming how we create, connect, and captivate.

a) Enhancing Personalization Through Data Analysis

At the heart of AI's impact is one powerful ability: personalization. Imagine being able to speak to each of your customers as if they were sitting across the table from you—understanding their needs, their quirks, and their timing. With AI, that dream is becoming a reality.

By processing vast amounts of data—more than any human team could ever manage—AI can identify patterns, predict behaviours, and deliver content tailored precisely to each individual. Think about how Netflix recommends your next binge-worthy show or how Amazon knows what you need before you do. That's AI-driven personalization in action.

In the marketing world, this means smarter campaigns, better segmentation, and experiences that feel not just relevant but magical.

b) AI in Creative Content Generation

Now, let's go a step further. AI isn't just helping us understand people—it's helping us create for them. Tools like GPT-3, DALL·E, and other generative platforms are making it possible to generate copy, images, and even videos with astonishing creativity and speed.

Of course, this doesn't mean machines are replacing human creativity, far from it. What it means is that we, as creatives, are gaining powerful allies—tools that can handle the heavy lifting, spark new ideas, and give us more space to do what we do best: tell stories that resonate.

Whether it's automating product descriptions, generating social media visuals, or helping brainstorm headlines, AI is helping teams do more faster—and sometimes, better.

c) AI-Powered Marketing Automation

Let's not forget the magic of automation. AI is taking over repetitive, time-consuming tasks—things like scheduling posts, personalizing emails, and even optimizing ad spend in real time. That's not just efficient; it's liberating.

Imagine having a system that knows when your audience is most likely to engage and sends content at that exact moment. Or a chatbot that provides round-the-clock support, making every customer feel heard and helped. These aren't futuristic fantasies—they're here, now, and evolving rapidly.

The more AI matures, the more creative teams can shift their energy from logistics to strategy. That's where the real magic happens.

3. Marketing in the Metaverse: Opportunities and Challenges

Now, let's step into something a bit more surreal—the metaverse. It's immersive. It's evolving. It's messy. And it's one of the most exciting frontiers marketing has ever seen.

a) *Opportunities for Immersive Brand Experiences*

In the metaverse, imagination becomes interaction. It's not about passive consumption anymore—it's about full-on immersion. Brands can create entire worlds, host virtual events, sell digital goods, and build experiences that live outside the boundaries of traditional media.

Luxury brands like Gucci and Balenciaga are already experimenting with digital fashion for avatars sold in virtual spaces like Roblox. These aren't gimmicks— they're signals of a future where identity, community, and commerce blend in entirely new ways.

Imagine your brand hosting a launch event in a virtual arena or letting users try out products in 3D before buying. These aren't "what-ifs." They're next steps.

b) *Challenges of Marketing in the Metaverse*

Of course, no new frontier comes without its challenges. Creating content for VR, AR, and interactive platforms demands technical expertise and serious investment. Not every brand is ready for that leap.

And let's be honest—the metaverse is still taking shape. Adoption is uneven, platforms are fragmented, and the user experience can vary wildly. It's exciting, yes—but it's also uncertain.

There are also deeper concerns: Will these virtual spaces be inclusive? Will they be safe? Brands must tread thoughtfully, ensuring they create environments where all users feel welcome and protected.

c) Navigating the Ethical and Privacy Implications

Then there's the data—lots of it. Every interaction in the metaverse generates information. And while that data can be a goldmine for personalization, it also raises serious questions around privacy, consent, and security.

As marketers, we must lead with integrity. That means being crystal clear about how we collect and use data, ensuring we uphold the highest standards of privacy, and staying vigilant about evolving regulations.

Because here's the truth: in the metaverse, as in the real world, trust is everything.

The next wave of global marketing isn't a distant storm on the horizon—it's already lapping at our shores. Sustainability, AI, and the metaverse are reshaping our work and our world. But at the core of it all remains something timeless: the human connection.

As we move forward, let's not just chase trends. Let's lead with purpose. Let's build with heart. And let's never forget that behind every screen, every click, every avatar, there's a person waiting to be seen, heard, and inspired.

Creative Corridors Around the World

If you've ever walked the streets of Berlin, felt the electric energy pulsing through Times Square, or heard the thunderous chaos of Mumbai's local trains. At the same time, ads flash from every corner, and then you've already brushed up against the heartbeat of global creativity. These cities aren't just places. They're experiences. Living, breathing hubs of imagination, technology, tradition, and disruption. They've built bridges between cultures and industries, between storytelling and strategy. Today, I want to take you on a journey through these creative corridors—not just to admire them but to learn from them, to see what they're doing differently, and perhaps most importantly, to understand how we, too, can build creative ecosystems that span borders and transform industries.

1. Exploring Other Creative Hubs: Berlin, New York, Mumbai

a) Berlin: The Epicenter of Tech-Driven Creativity

Berlin doesn't just hum with innovation—it roars. It's a place where artists and coders sip espresso side by side, where historic scars live alongside futuristic dreams. Walking through Kreuzberg or Mitte, you'll quickly realise that creativity here isn't reserved for galleries—it's in the air, in the apps being coded at cafés, and in the immersive pop-ups lighting up industrial spaces by night.

Berlin, often dubbed Europe's creative heartbeat, is more than a city—it's a mindset. There's a rawness here, an openness, a rebellious spirit that embraces the unconventional. And that spirit fuels an ever-evolving creative economy. Startups flourish in repurposed warehouses. Young visionaries with wild ideas find room— affordably, compared to cities like London or Paris—to breathe life into them.

What truly sets Berlin apart is how seamlessly it weaves technology into artistry. Augmented reality? Virtual reality? Interactive digital installations? They're not gimmicks here—they're the canvas. Marketing agencies don't just sell stories— they build them in code, wireframes, and pixels. They craft experiences. Ones that linger. Ones that move.

Berlin's campaigns aren't merely disruptive—they're immersive. They speak to a generation raised on digital, one that demands more than attention—they want emotion, participation, and purpose. It's no wonder Berlin has emerged as a leader in crafting global campaigns for digitally native audiences. If you're a brand looking to push boundaries, Berlin shows us how the line between art and algorithm can beautifully blur.

b) New York: The Global Marketing Powerhouse

Ah, New York. The city that never sleeps—because it's too busy creating the next big thing. There's a reason why the world calls it the capital of marketing. It's not just the skyscrapers, the Wall Street deals, or the fashion runways. It's the energy. It's the noise—the kind that fuels adrenaline and forces ideas to move faster, hit harder, and shine brighter.

Here, marketing isn't just a career—it's a culture. You feel it in every subway ad, every Times Square billboard, every digital activation pulsing through Madison Avenue. Home to legends like Ogilvy, BBDO, and Droga5, New York has long dictated the rhythm of global campaigns.

But it's not resting on its laurels. This city has evolved. It's embraced data not as a replacement for creativity but as a co-pilot. It tests, it tweaks, it iterates. Campaigns here don't just look good—they work. They perform. They deliver because behind every powerful visual is a mountain of insight, analytics, and audience empathy.

And then there's the people. Oh, the people. They come from everywhere, bringing their cultures, their languages, their stories. New York is a melting pot in the truest sense, and that diversity breathes life into its marketing. Campaigns here aren't just for America—they're built to resonate with the world. Whether it's a luxury brand targeting Tokyo or a non-profit campaign reaching Nairobi, NYC knows how to speak the language of global hearts.

c) Mumbai: The Heart of India's Creative Revolution

Mumbai. Just saying the name brings a rhythm to the tongue, doesn't it? It's a city of contrasts—of towering skyscrapers shadowing ancient temples, of traditional street vendors setting up next to cutting-edge co-working spaces. It's a place where storytelling is not a skill—it's a way of life.

Mumbai doesn't just advertise—it narrates. And that comes as no surprise when you consider it's the beating heart of Bollywood. Here, emotion is currency. And when brands tap into that cinematic tradition, something magical happens. They don't just promote products—they create moments that stir souls, trigger nostalgia, and bring tears to their eyes.

But Mumbai isn't stuck in the past. Far from it. It's embracing digital transformation with a hunger that's inspiring. Fueled by a young, tech-savvy population and one of the fastest-growing internet markets in the world, Mumbai's marketing landscape is in full bloom. Influencer campaigns? Mobile-first storytelling? Regional content tailored for hyper-local relevance? It's all here— and it's exploding with potential.

What's especially beautiful about Mumbai is its balance. It doesn't discard tradition to make room for innovation. It holds both in its hands—like a filmmaker who reveres folklore but shoots in 4K. This city reminds us that authenticity and advancement don't have to be opposing forces. In fact, when they dance together, they create something truly unforgettable.

2. What Can We Learn from Other Global Marketing Centers?

You might be wondering, "What do these creative giants have to do with me?" The answer? Everything. Because the lessons they offer aren't limited by geography. They're universal. They're human. And they give us a blueprint for what's possible when creativity is nurtured with courage and intention.

a) Berlin's Focus on Technology-Driven Creativity

Berlin teaches us to stop seeing technology as a tool and start seeing it as a medium. It's not just about using VR to be flashy—it's about using VR to immerse. To connect. To make your audience feel like they're part of the story. We need to think beyond static visuals. We need to build experiences. Interactive. Emotional. Real.

Berlin reminds us that it's okay—no, essential—to experiment. To try, to fail, to iterate. That's how innovation happens. And if we want to stay ahead in this fast-paced world, we have to embrace the unknown and invite tech into the creative room—not as a guest, but as a co-creator.

b) New York's Data-Driven Creativity and Global Mindset

New York shows us how data and creativity are not enemies—
they're soulmates. When we understand our audience deeply, when we
know what makes them laugh, cry, or click, we can craft stories that aren't
just beautiful but impactful. Stories that land. Stories that stick.

And more importantly, New York reminds us to think globally. To
look beyond our zip codes. To understand that creativity is not a
language—it's a feeling. And feelings cross borders. When we embrace
diversity, when we bring multicultural voices into the room, we don't
just make better marketing—we make better connections.

c) Mumbai's Blend of Tradition and Modernity

Mumbai teaches us the power of "and." You can be modern *and*
rooted. You can be digital *and* human. You can honour culture *and*
explore the cutting edge. We don't have to choose. The best campaigns,
the ones that go viral, that go deep— they blend the familiar with the
fresh. The timeless with the trending.

Mumbai shows us that local is not small. It's powerful. It's specific.
And when you speak to people in their language, in their rhythm, on their
terms—they listen. They engage. They believe.

3. Building a Creative Network Across Borders

So, how do we take all this and turn it into action? How do we build
our own global creative corridor—one that connects talent, ideas, and
purpose across oceans?

a) Foster Cross-Cultural Collaboration

Start by reaching out. Talk to creators who don't look like you, think
like you, or live where you do. Use platforms that connect creatives
across countries. Attend global summits, even virtually. Join
communities. When you bring different voices to the table, the table gets
richer. The ideas are bolder. The results are better.

b) Leverage Global Talent Pools

Remote work has made the world smaller. You don't need to hire locals to build local relevance. There's a designer in São Paulo, a copywriter in Lagos, and a strategist in Seoul waiting to help you see your campaign through a different lens. Build diverse teams not just for optics but for impact.

c) Engage with Local Influencers and Creatives

Influencers aren't just trendsetters—they're culture carriers. They know their communities better than any algorithm ever will. Partner with them. Listen to them. Let them guide you into the hearts of your audiences. And don't just see them as channels—see them as collaborators.

In Closing…

Berlin. New York. Mumbai. Three cities. Three cultures. Infinite inspiration.

But here's the truth—your city, your studio, your team can be the next creative corridor. All it takes is intention, empathy, and courage. Creativity doesn't belong to capitals. It belongs to those bold enough to build it.

So, let's build. Together.

Section 3: Becoming a Leader in the Creative Corridor

Let me tell you something I've learned on this journey: the creative economy isn't just another business trend—it's alive. It breathes, evolves, and pulses with the energy of millions of passionate minds chasing possibility. It's where ideas don't just sell; they shape cultures, redefine industries, and awaken something inside us that refuses to settle for the ordinary.

You see it in the electric atmosphere of London's creative alleys, in the edgy grit of Berlin's start-up districts, in the relentless hum of New York's marketing agencies, and in the vibrant chaos of Mumbai's media houses. The creative corridors of the world are buzzing. And somewhere in the noise, there's room for you—not just to belong, but to lead.

Becoming a leader in this space isn't a title you earn once. It's a role you grow into every single day—with every challenge, every reinvention, every act of courage. So, let's walk through what it really takes to rise and lead in this ever-changing, wildly beautiful economy.

1. How to Make Your Mark in the Creative Economy

Talent, while essential, is just the starting point. It's like having the raw ingredients for a great dish, but it's the preparation, the vision, and the execution that truly make it memorable. To make your mark in the world of creativity, you need to go beyond raw talent. You need to learn how to be both an artist and an architect.

Think of it this way: creativity is the canvas, but it's your ability to design, structure, and build something with purpose that turns it into something meaningful. It's not enough to simply have a brilliant idea—you have to know how to take that idea, shape it, mould it, and guide it toward a clear goal. Whether you're crafting a marketing campaign, designing a product, or telling a brand story, it's the combination of vision and strategy that will define your success.

Being an artist means embracing the freedom to explore, experiment, and dream big. But being an architect means knowing how to take those dreams and turn them into something real—something tangible that connects with people, resonates with audiences, and leaves a lasting impression. It's this balance between creativity and structure, between passion and purpose, that will truly allow you to stand out in the world of global marketing.

In this journey, you're not just creating for the sake of creating—you're building with intention. You're crafting something that not only showcases your talent but also serves a larger purpose, speaks to your audience, and leaves an impact. And that's what makes creativity powerful. It's not just about what you can create—it's about what you can build with it.

a) Develop a Unique Value Proposition

In a world teeming with talent, how do you stand out?

You start by getting honest with yourself. What makes you, well... you? Your story, your lens, your strange mix of skills—that's your gold. Whether you're a digital artist with a knack for data or a marketer with a love for storytelling, it's your blend that carves out your value proposition.

I remember grappling with this early in my career. I wasn't just a marketer—I was someone who understood analytics as much as aesthetics. That fusion became my advantage. Your edge might be different, but trust me, it's there. You just have to uncover it and communicate it clearly. Own your lane and make it unforgettable.

b) Network and Build Relationships

Now, here's a truth I wish someone had told me sooner—your connections will shape your direction.

Not the superficial kind of networking that ends with a business card and a forgettable smile. I'm talking about real human relationships. The kind is built on curiosity, respect, and shared values.

Go where your people are. Attend events, join communities, and collaborate without expectations. Reach out to people who inspire you—not just for what they know, but for how they make others feel. And remember: a kind word, a thoughtful comment, a moment of vulnerability—these can spark connections that open doors you never even saw.

c) Create and Share Your Work Publicly

I know it's scary. Putting your work out there feels like opening your diary to the world. But in the creative economy, invisibility is the real risk.

Start small. Post your thoughts. Publish that article. Share your creative process. Let people see your evolution, not just your polished end product. The goal isn't perfection—it's connection. The more you show up, the more chances you have to be seen, heard, and remembered.

Your voice matters. Say it out loud.

d) Embrace Innovation and Risk-Taking

Being in the creative economy means you're walking a path that hasn't been paved yet. Innovation isn't optional—it's your oxygen.

Try new formats. Play with emerging tech. Experiment with bold campaigns. Sure, you might fall flat sometimes. But failure here isn't a full stop—it's a comma. It's feedback, not finality.

Look at the greatest creative leaders—they didn't get there by playing it safe. They leapt into the unknown, armed with curiosity and the willingness to get it wrong before they got it right.

2. The Importance of Lifelong Learning and Adaptation

The moment you believe you've *arrived*—the moment you start thinking that you know it all or that you've mastered everything there is to know—that's when you start falling behind.

It's a harsh truth, but it's one, that's crucial to grasp if you want to truly thrive in today's fast-paced, ever-evolving world. The landscape of business, technology, and creativity doesn't stay stagnant; it doesn't wait for anyone. It moves fast. It adapts. And if you're not continually learning, growing, and adjusting, you'll find yourself left behind, stuck in yesterday's mindset while everyone else moves forward.

In this world, staying relevant is not a passive act. It's not something that happens by default. It's an active choice—a mindset. To stay relevant, you must stay curious. You have to have that hunger, that fire inside you, to keep seeking out new knowledge, new perspectives, and new ways of doing things. This curiosity, this drive to never stop learning, is what will allow you to stay ahead of the curve. It's what will fuel your creativity, your innovation, and your ability to adapt to an ever-changing environment.

Lifelong learning is not just a nice-to-have. It's a must. The world is constantly changing, and to remain a leader in your field, you need to be in tune with those changes. Whether it's mastering a new tool, exploring a new concept, or adapting to a new trend, the ability to learn and adapt is what separates the successful from the stagnant.

But let's be clear about one thing: lifelong learning doesn't just mean formal education or taking another course (though those are important, too). It's about continuously expanding your knowledge in all areas of your life. It's about reading books, seeking out mentors, attending workshops, and, yes, sometimes even learning from your failures. It's about being open to new ideas and recognizing that the more you learn, the more you realize you don't know. That's where growth happens.

The most successful people in any field are the ones who never stop asking questions. They are the ones who are always looking for ways to improve, to refine their skills, and to expand their knowledge. They understand that expertise is not a destination but a journey—a journey that requires constant attention and effort.

In addition to knowledge, adaptability is just as critical. In today's world, things change in an instant—technology evolves, industries shift, trends come and go. If you're not willing to adapt, to evolve with the times, then you risk becoming obsolete. The world won't wait for you to catch up, and opportunities won't wait for you to get on board. To thrive, you must be able to pivot when needed, to adjust your approach, and to embrace change.

Adapting also means being open to feedback. Constructive criticism can be one of the most valuable tools for growth, yet many people avoid it because it's uncomfortable. But if you can shift your mindset to view feedback as an opportunity for improvement rather than a personal attack, it becomes a catalyst for your development. Ask questions. Seek advice. Don't be afraid to challenge your own assumptions. The best leaders are those who aren't afraid to admit they don't have all the answers—and who actively seek out the knowledge they need to continue growing.

This mindset of lifelong learning and adaptability will not only help you stay relevant but it will also keep your passion alive. When you're constantly learning and growing, your work doesn't become stagnant. It remains fresh, exciting, and full of possibility. You become someone who's not just keeping up with the times but actively shaping the future.

The key to success is not static—it's dynamic. It's about knowing that you're never done. There's always more to learn, more to explore, more to create. It's about embracing change and seeing every challenge as an opportunity to learn, adapt, and grow. The most successful people don't just *adapt* to change—they *lead* change. And that's what you can do, too.

So, here's the challenge: commit to a mindset of continuous learning and growth. Never stop questioning, never stop exploring, and never stop evolving. The world moves fast, but so can you—if you stay curious and embrace the process of learning and adapting. Your journey of growth never ends, and that's what makes it so exciting. The possibilities are endless, and you have the power to shape your future, one step of learning at a time.

a) Stay Curious and Embrace Change

I'll be honest—change is uncomfortable. It disrupts routines and shakes your confidence. But it's also the secret to staying ahead. When you stay curious, you're not just reacting to change—you're leading it.

Read voraciously. Watch how trends evolve. Ask questions no one else is asking. The best creative minds don't just consume—they observe, question, and connect dots others can't see yet.

Let go of the fear of looking foolish. Trust me, some of my best ideas came from wandering off the beaten path, following a hunch, and piecing together inspiration from the most unexpected places.

b) Invest in Personal Development

Your technical skills will open doors, but your personal growth will determine how far you walk through them.

Build emotional intelligence. Learn how to manage yourself in moments of stress. Understand what drives people, not just what sells to them. These "soft" skills are actually power tools.

Reflect on your strengths and shadows. Ask for feedback, even when it stings. The version of you that succeeds in the creative corridor isn't just talented—it's self-aware, resilient, and endlessly evolving.

c) Keep Abreast of New Technologies and Methodologies

Technology isn't here to replace your creativity—it's here to amplify it.

Don't be intimidated. Get curious about AI, explore blockchain applications, and dive into data. These are not just tech buzzwords—they're creative catalysts. When you learn to speak both the language of imagination and the language of innovation, you become unstoppable.

Think of these tools not as threats but as creative collaborators. Used right, they can take your storytelling, branding, and campaigns to levels you never imagined.

3. Leaving a Lasting Legacy in Global Marketing

This, to me, is the heart of leadership. It's not just about what you build—it's about what you leave behind.

a) Mentorship and Giving Back

Someone once believed in me when I wasn't sure I believed in myself. That moment changed everything.

Now, I try to pay it forward—and I encourage you to do the same. Mentor someone. Answer that DM from a student. Share your insights with generosity. You never know the ripple effect your words might create.

Leadership isn't a solo journey. It's a torch passed hand-to-hand. By lifting others, you don't just leave a mark—you start a movement.

b) Create Work That Endures

Trends fade. Algorithms shift. But meaningful work? That echoes.

Strive to create campaigns, brands, and content that resonate long after the spotlight moves on. Work that stirs something real. Work that reflects your values, not just market trends.

Ask yourself, "Will this matter five years from now?" If the answer is yes, you're building a legacy, not just visibility.

c) Contribute to Thought Leadership

Your experiences—yes, yours—are worthy of being shared.

Write that book. Speak on that panel. Share your perspective on a podcast. Every time you share your truth, you invite others to see the world differently. That's not just thought leadership—it's soul leadership.

You don't have to wait until you "arrive." Your voice, your story, and your ideas are valid right now.

As we bring this journey to a close, let me leave you with this: becoming a leader in the creative corridor isn't about being the loudest voice in the room. It's about being the one who listens deeply, creates boldly, and leads with heart.

You don't need to have it all figured out. Just start where you are. Grow. Connect. Learn. Share. Fail and rise again. And know that in doing so, you're not just participating in the creative economy—you're shaping it.

The world doesn't need more perfect leaders. It needs real ones. Human ones. Creative ones.

And maybe, just maybe, it needs you.

As we reach the end of this journey together, I can't help but reflect on how far we've come. What began as a collection of thoughts, insights, and experiences has now transformed into something much larger—something that, I hope, has sparked new ideas, inspired deeper thinking, and, most importantly, connected with you on a human level.

When I started writing this book, I wasn't just thinking about marketing trends, strategies, or creative technologies. I was thinking about you—the marketer, the strategist, the creator, and the dreamer—who is navigating this ever-changing landscape. I wanted to offer something that was more than just theory. I wanted to share the heart and soul of marketing, the human side of the industry that so often gets lost in metrics and data. Because at the end of the day, it's not just about numbers or algorithms—it's about people. It's about understanding what makes us tick, what drives us, and how we can connect with one another in a world that is both vast and deeply personal.

As you turn the final page, I hope you're leaving with more than just knowledge. I hope you're leaving with a renewed sense of purpose, a deeper understanding of the power of creativity, and a belief in the transformative potential of marketing. This is a field that's full of possibilities, yes, but it's also full of heart—stories waiting to be told, brands waiting to be built, and connections waiting to be made.

The journey doesn't end here. In fact, it's just beginning. The world of global marketing is constantly evolving, and the possibilities for what you can create are limitless. I hope you feel inspired to take the tools, the insights, and the stories shared in this book and make them your own. Because at the end of the day, it's not just about what we create—it's about how we make others feel, how we connect with them, and how we inspire them to see the world in a new light.

Thank you for coming on this journey with me. Let's keep pushing the boundaries, staying curious, and, most importantly—let's keep creating.

The world is waiting for your next great idea.